Jean hee's
BEST OF THE BEST

HAWAI'I
RECIPES

MUTUAL PUBLISHING

Library of Congress Cataloging-in-Publication Data

Hee, Jean Watanabe.
Jean Hee's best of the best Hawai'i recipes.
    p. cm.
ISBN 1-56647-842-1 (softcover : alk. paper)
1. Hawaiian cookery. I. Title. II. Title: Best of the best Hawaii's
recipes.
TX724.5.H3H446 2007
641.59969--dc22
                                        2007026485

                ISBN-10: 1-56647-842-1
                ISBN-13: 978-1-56647-842-7

            First Printing, September 2007
            Second Printing, March 2008

                Mutual Publishing, LLC
            1215 Center Street, Suite 210
            Honolulu, Hawai'i 96816
        Ph: 808-732-1709 / Fax: 808-734-4094
            email: info@mutualpublishing.com
                www.mutualpublishing.com

                Printed in Korea

Dedication

To my mother, Asae Watanabe,
who celebrated her 88th birthday this year.

Table of Contents

Recipes with * are *Quick and Easy*

Acknowledgments x
Introduction xi

PŪPŪ
'Ahi Limu Poke...2
Shoyu Poke...3
7-Layer Dip 3
Curry Mango Cream Cheese Spread 4
Clam Dip 5
Guacamole..6
Barbecue Sticks 7
Spinach Dip 8
Spring Rolls..9
Buffalo Wings...10
Sesame Seed Chicken 11
Cocktail Shrimp...12
Furikake Seared 'Ahi 13
Spinach Rolls..13
Mimi's Shrimp..14
Oyster Bacon Wrap..15
Shrimp Lumpia..16
Crispy Gau Gee 17
Stuffed Aburage with Somen 18

SALADS
Broccoli Salad 20
Pasta Salad...21
Bean Salad..22
Broccoli Shrimp Salad..23
Chinese Chicken Salad 24
Pine Nut Salad 25
Soba Salad..26
Spinach Salad with Hot Dressing......................................27
Strawberry Salad..28
Taegu Ocean Salad Linguine..29
Tofu Salad..30
Potato and Macaroni Salad 31
24-Hour Lettuce Salad 32

SIDES
Baked Beans 34
Scalloped Potatoes...34
Choi Sum...35

Green Bean Casserole 36
Kinpira Gobo with Portuguese Sausage 37
Namul 38
Nishime 39
Ong Choy and Harm Ha (Shrimp Sauce) 40
Cucumber Namasu 41
Takuan 42
Roasted Vegetables 43
Gon Lo Mein 44

SOUPS
Mushroom Soup 46
Black Bean Soup 47
Watercress Egg-Drop Soup 47
Chinese Cabbage Soup 48
Country Comfort Corn Chowder 49
Hearty Miso Soup 50
Hot and Sour Soup 51
Jook (Chinese Rice Porridge) 52
Imitation Bird Nest Soup 53
Minestrone Soup 54
Oxtail Soup 55
Portuguese Bean Soup 56
Seafood Bisque 57
Turkey Chowder 58
Kim Chee Soup 59
Won Ton Soup 60

MAIN DISHES
Beef Broccoli 62
Beef Tomato 63
Corned Beef Hash Patties 64
Jumbo's Restaurant's Beef Stew 65
Sukiyaki 66
Stuffed Cabbage Rolls 67
Easy Pot Roast 68
Lasagna 69
No-Fail Roast Beef 70
DeLuz Vindha D'Ahlos Roast 71
Roast Lamb 72
Lazy-Style Laulau 73
* Tonkatsu 74
Sari Sari 75
Black Bean Spareribs 76
Sweet-Sour Spareribs 77
Pork Hash 78

Miso Pork Roast 79
Roast Pork 80
* Mushroom Pork Chops 80
Pork-Tofu Casserole 81
Ma Po Tofu (Pork Tofu)..82
Chicken Cacciatore..83
Cashew Chicken 84
Chicken Chili..85
Chicken Enchilada...86
Chicken Adobo 87
* Chicken Katsu..88
Flavored Chicken for Chinese Stir-fry 89
Chicken Long Rice 90
Gay's Easy Potluck Chicken 91
Yakitori...91
Fried Chicken 92
Cold Chicken with Ginger Sauce...93
Lemon Chicken...94
Shoyu Chicken..95
Easy Roast Chicken 95
Mochiko Chicken...96
McCarthy's Marinade 97
Butter Yaki...98
Baked Fish 99
Miso Butterfish...99
Honey-Glazed Walnut Shrimp 100
'Ōpakapaka with Chinese Cabbage....................................101
Chinese Steamed Fish..102
Shrimp Curry 103
* Butterfish with Shoyu Sauce..104
Easy Seafood Pasta 105
* Furikake Salmon..106
Shrimp with Black Bean Sauce..107
Spanish Rice 108
Tofu Burgers 109
Oriental-Style Fish...109
Stuffed Tofu 110

DESSERTS
Chocolate Banana Bread..112
Watergate Cake..113
Bacardi® Rum Cake..114
Cocoa Cake...115
Chiffon Cake..116
Kahlúa® Cake...117
Mango Bread 118
Carrot Cake...119

Corn Bread 120
Creamsicle Cake 121
Poppy Seed Bundt Cake..122
Sour Cream Chocolate Cake 122
Mandarin Peach Cake 123
Pumpkin Crunch 124
Pineapple Upside-Down Cake...125
Arare Cookie Crunch 125
Moist Banana Cake...126
Chocolate Delight 127
Fresh Mango Pie 128
Banana Cream Delight...129
Lemon Meringue Pie 130
Okinawan Sweet Potato Pie with Haupia Topping 131
No-Fail Pie Crust 132
Shortbread Cookies...132
Tofu Pie 133
Pumpkin Custard Pie 134
Haupia Chocolate Pie 135
Kona Coffee Mud Pie 136
Blueberry Cream Cheese Pie 137
Irresistible Peanut Butter Cookies.....................................138
Sponge Drops 139
Sugar Cookies...140
Furikake Chex® Mix 141
Lemon Bars 142
Hawaiian Chocolate Chip Cookies.....................................143
Old-Fashioned Oatmeal Cookies 144
Almond Cookies 145
Andagi 146
Almond Float..147
Blueberry Mochi...147
Goodie Goodie Dessert...148
King's Hawaiian® Sweet Bread–Bread Pudding 148
Rainbow Finger Jell-O® 149
Tri-Colored Mochi..150
Moist Chocolate Cake...151
Broken Glass Dessert..152
Coconut Butter Mochi 153
Fruitcake Bars...154
Melt 'em Cookies 155
Energy Bars with Fruits 156
Zucchini Cake...158

Glossary..159
Index...161

Acknowledgments

I want to thank all my relatives, neighbors, and friends who contributed their best and favorite recipes. It was difficult to select the best of any dish since each individual has his own preference, but I tried to get as many responses as I could for the final selection. I thank all the people who taste-tested and gave me their opinions.

I want to especially thank my husband, Don, who is my greatest supporter and who has had to live through the hundreds of recipe tests.

Finally, I want to thank my publisher, Bennett Hymer, for his support and encouragement. Thank you to all the helpful and friendly staff at Mutual Publishing.

Introduction

This cookbook was suggested to me—and requested by others—as a great way to compile into one book the best local recipes from my five specialty cookbooks. It would be a handy resource for the busy mother, young couple, the college student living away from home, or for anyone who wants to cook more at home.

We live in a fast-food society. It is so easy to order a meal "to go" from any of our many take-out places. With a variety of wonderful ethnic restaurants here in Hawai'i, we could eat out seven days a week and enjoy quite diverse tastes. However, there are many advantages to preparing your own meals. Besides being healthier and more economical, I think it's more relaxing for a family to eat together at home. It helps to build closer relationships with each other. There's also great satisfaction in preparing a meal for your loved ones. Recipes can be adjusted to suit individual tastes and allows your creativity to blossom.

This cookbook is user-friendly. I have written the recipes as clearly and simply as possible. My selections, or best picks for this cookbook, are focused on easy-to-follow local recipes with great results. There are some recipes which require a bit more work, but are worth the effort. For those who have all of my cookbooks, you will find some great new recipes that yield great results.

Pūpū

'Ahi Limu Poke

yield: 4 – 6 appetizer servings

* *

1 pound 'ahi, cut into bite-sized pieces
1/4 cup green onion, finely chopped
1 small Maui onion, finely sliced
1/2 cup limu, roughly chopped
1/2 teaspoon sesame oil, adjust to taste
Hawaiian salt, to taste
chili pepper water, to taste or use chili pepper seeds
1/2 teaspoon kukui nut ('inamona), to taste (optional)

Combine all ingredients and mix well. Adjust seasonings. Refrigerate.

Chili pepper water:
1 quart water
2 Tablespoons Hawaiian salt
2 to 3 dry Hawaiian chili peppers

Boil water. Add salt and stir to dissolve. Remove from heat and let stand until cool. Rinse peppers and place in glass jar. Add salt water. Let stand for one day. Store in refrigerator. (Serve with lomi salmon, poke, and stew.)

Shoyu Poke

yield: 4 – 6 appetizer servings

✳ ✳

1 pound aku, cut in bite-sized pieces
1/4 cup green onion, chopped
1/2 teaspoon roasted sesame seeds
1/4 cup soy sauce
1 teaspoon fresh ginger, grated
1/2 teaspoon 'inamona (optional)
1 Hawaiian chili pepper, seeded and minced

Combine all ingredients and mix well. Chill before serving.

7-Layer Dip

yield: 12–15 servings

✳ ✳

1 can refried beans (12- to 16-oz.)
1 carton sour cream (8-oz.)
1 carton avocado dip (8-oz.)
1 cup or more Cheddar cheese
1 can mild chili salsa (7-oz.)
1 can olives (5-oz.), sliced
1 large tomato, diced

Layer ingredients in order listed in 9 × 13 pan or in 2 smaller serving dishes. Cover with plastic wrap and refrigerate. Serve with crackers or tortilla chips.

Note: This is another favorite that's been around for a long time!

Curry Mango Cream Cheese Spread

yield: 6 – 8 servings

* *

2 packages cream cheese (8-oz. each), softened
1-1/2 teaspoons curry powder
1/2 teaspoon dry mustard powder
1/2 cup mango chutney (Major Grey's Chutney brand
   recommended)
2 teaspoons green onion, chopped, green part only (optional)
1/4 cup sliced toasted almonds
1 box crackers (e.g., Carr's® water crackers, Ritz® crackers)

Place cream cheese in large bowl to soften; set aside. Mix together curry powder and dry mustard. Mix in mango chutney. Add to softened cream cheese; mix together thoroughly.

In medium-size plastic container with lid, sprinkle almonds and green onions on bottom of container. Spread curry cream cheese mixture over green onions and almonds. Cover with lid and refrigerate for at least one hour. Use butter knife to loosen mold from around the sides of container. Place serving plate on top of container and turn over. Serve with crackers.

Note: This is one of those spreads that is such a great hit at parties and the recipe is passed on from friend to friend. It not only tastes great but also displays nicely. Thank you to Faye Lynn Au for sharing this recipe. This spread is also great with Tandoori Chicken.

Clam Dip

yield: 1-1/2 cups

* *

1 package cream cheese (8-oz.)
1 can minced clams (7.5-oz.); drained, juice reserved
1 Tablespoon onion, finely minced
1 heaping Tablespoon mayonnaise
1 teaspoon lemon juice
salt and pepper to taste
Worcestershire® sauce, to taste (optional)

Leave cream cheese at room temperature to soften. Blend cream cheese, mayonnaise, and enough clam juice for good dipping consistency. Add rest of ingredients. Chill. Serve with potato chips.

Note: Family and friends have been using this favorite dip ever since we got this recipe from Jean Tanimoto about 30 years ago!

Guacamole

yield: about 1 cup

* *

1 large ripe avocado, peeled and pitted
1/2 cup onion, finely chopped (adjust to taste)
1/2 tomato, seeded and diced
1 teaspoon lemon juice
1 Tablespoon mayonnaise
1/2 teaspoon salt
1/2 teaspoon chili powder
1 teaspoon Worcestershire® sauce
Tabasco® sauce, to taste

Mash avocados to a coarse texture. Add rest of ingredients and mix thoroughly. Cover and refrigerate 30 to 60 minutes before serving.

Note: When covering guacamole, place plastic wrap directly on dip to keep color fresh. Mix just before serving.

Barbecue Sticks

yield: about 30 sticks

* *

**2 pounds boneless crossrib roast, cut into 1/4-inch slices
(ask butcher to do this)
30 bamboo skewers (8 inches long), soaked in water**

**Marinade:
1 cup soy sauce
3/4 cup sugar
1/8 cup water
1/2 inch fresh ginger, grated
1 clove garlic, crushed**

Combine marinade ingredients. Cut meat slices into strips about 1-inch wide. Soak in marinade for about 30 minutes. String strips onto skewers in an undulating style. Grill on hibachi.

Note: Remember the wonderful smell of teriyaki meat being grilled and eating barbecue sticks at school carnivals? Somehow skewering the strips of teriyaki beef makes it even juicier and tastier.

Spinach Dip

yield: 4-1/2 cups

* *

**2 boxes frozen chopped spinach (10-oz. each), thawed and
squeezed dry
1 container sour cream (16-oz.)
1 cup mayonnaise
1 envelope Liption® Onion Soup and Dip Mix
1 can minced clams (6.5-oz.), drained
1 can water chestnuts (8-oz.), drained and finely chopped
2 stalks green onion, minced (optional)**

Mix all ingredients well; chill. Serve with crackers, cottage
bread or vegetables.

Suggestion: Carve out center of round loaf of French bread.
Cube excess bread to use as "dippers." Pour spinach dip into
the center of bread. Bread can eventually be torn apart and
eaten.

*Note: What makes this the best spinach dip is the minced
clams added to it. I love this with Ritz® crackers!*

Spring Rolls

yield: 8–10 appetizer servings

* *

1 package Menlo® Lumpia Wrap (16-oz.), 30 wrappers
1 pound ground beef (or pork or chicken)
2 Tablespoons oil
1 package chop suey vegetables (9-oz.)
1 package long rice (2-oz.)
2 eggs, slightly beaten
1 small onion, minced
1 package imitation crab (about 1/2 pound), coarsely
    shredded
1 Tablespoon oyster sauce
pepper and salt, to taste
garlic powder, to taste
oil for deep-frying

Defrost lumpia wrappers in refrigerator a day before using.

Soak long rice in water for 10 minutes. Cut in 1-inch lengths; set aside. Heat oil in frying pan; sauté onion. Add ground beef and rest of ingredients (except lumpia wrappers and oil). Cook together until bean sprouts are done but not limp.

Place one tablespoonful of mixture onto lumpia. Wrap envelope-style and seal by wetting the last edge. Deep-fry in medium-hot oil until lightly browned. Drain on paper towels.

Serve with Vietnamese Lumpia Sauce (see recipe on page 16).

Buffalo Wings

yield: 12–18 pieces

* *

12 to 18 chicken wings
1/2 cup flour
1/4 teaspoon salt
1/4 teaspoon cayenne pepper
1/4 teaspoon paprika

Combine flour, salt, cayenne pepper, and paprika; place in plastic bag. Add chicken wings and shake to coat evenly. Refrigerate wings for about an hour. Remove from refrigerator and let sit 30 minutes before cooking.

1/4 cup butter
1/4 cup hot sauce (e.g., Red Devil Cayenne Pepper Sauce)
1/4 teaspoon garlic, grated
oil for deep-frying

Melt butter and mix in hot sauce and garlic; set aside.

Heat oil to 350°F and fry chicken wings for about 10 minutes, or until dark brown. Remove and pour hot sauce over and stir.

Suggestion: Serve with celery sticks and bleu cheese or ranch dressing.

Note: I got this recipe from someone who got it based on a well-known restaurant's buffalo wings. Fantastic taste!

Sesame Seed Chicken

yield: 6–8 appetizer servings

* *

2 to 3 pounds chicken drumettes
oil for deep-frying

Marinade:
4 Tablespoons flour
8 Tablespoons cornstarch
4 Tablespoons sugar
1-1/2 teaspoons salt
5 Tablespoons soy sauce
2 eggs
2 cloves garlic, minced
1 stalk green onion, chopped
2 Tablespoons sesame seeds

Mix marinade ingredients until well blended. Marinate chicken overnight in refrigerator, stirring occasionally. Heat oil and deep-fry chicken. Drain on paper towels.

Note: Whenever Jennifer comes back to Hawai'i, she goes to her favorite okazu place where she always orders sesame chicken. She asked me for a recipe like it. After testing several recipes, she finally said, "This is it!" It was Grandma Watanabe's old recipe.

Cocktail Shrimp

yield: 50–60 pieces

* *

2 quarts water
1 bay leaf
juice of one lemon
rind of one lemon
1 can beer
2 pounds shrimp (31- to 40-count), peeled and deveined

Combine all ingredients (except shrimp) and bring water to aggressive boil. Add shrimp and stir, whirling through the boiling water. Cover tightly and remove from heat. Allow to stand for 5 minutes exactly. Then drain through colander. Run shrimp under cold water to cool. Chill and arrange on platter with dipping sauce.

Dipping Sauce:
1 cup catsup
2 teaspoons wasabi paste
juice of one lemon

Note: From 1 to 5 pounds of shrimp may be used with this recipe. This is definitely for shrimp lovers. They're "crunchy, " cooked just right, with a light fresh taste. Our Popo just loves this shrimp! We like the 31- to 40-count best, but you can use the 26- to 30-count, if desired.

Furikake Seared ʻAhi

yield: 4–6 appetizer servings

* *

1 pound ʻahi fillet, sliced into pieces 3/4-inch thick
3 to 4 Tablespoons furikake for coating
2 to 3 teaspoons oil

Dipping Sauce:
2 Tablespoons soy sauce
wasabi, to taste

Coat ʻahi pieces with furikake. Sear ʻahi in hot oil in non-stick skillet on medium-high heat, keeping the middle raw. Slice ʻahi, sashimi style. Mix soy sauce and wasabi to desired taste and use as dipping sauce.

Spinach Rolls

yield: about 80 pieces

* *

2 boxes chopped spinach (10-oz. each), thawed and
    excess water squeezed out
1 container sour cream (8-oz.)
1 cup mayonnaise
1/2 cup bacon bits, (Hormel® Real Bacon Bits preferred)
1 package Hidden Valley® Original Ranch® Dressing (1-oz.)
1/4 cup green onion, chopped
1/4 cup water chestnuts, chopped
1 package flour tortillas (17.5-oz.), 10 soft taco-size tortillas

Mix together all ingredients (except tortillas) until completely blended. Divide mixture into 10 parts (about 1/3 cup each). Spread evenly on tortillas and roll. Wrap each roll individually in waxed paper. Refrigerate overnight in covered container or 3 hours in freezer prior to cutting for easier slicing. Trim ends before slicing, if desired. Slice into 8 pieces.

Mimi's Shrimp

yield: about 15 appetizer servings

* *

3 pounds shrimp (21- to 25-count)

Marinade:
1 cup canola oil
2 teaspoons soy sauce
3 Tablespoons honey
3 teaspoons Hawaiian salt (pulverized with mortar and pestle)
2 cloves garlic, grated
dash of Tabasco® sauce

Do not peel shrimp. Cut shrimp from back and remove vein. Butterfly shrimp and lay flat.

Mix together oil, soy sauce, honey, pulverized Hawaiian salt, and garlic. Add a few drops of Tabasco® sauce. Keep stirring mixture as you dip each shrimp in the marinade. Lay flat in a pan for 1 hour. Grill on hibachi.

Note: This is still the best-tasting grilled shrimp! Everyone loves this. Thank you, Mimi.

Oyster Bacon Wrap

yield: about 20–24 pieces

* *

2 jars fresh oysters (10-oz. each)
1 Tablespoon olive oil
4 cloves garlic, finely chopped
1 bunch fresh spinach, cleaned (or 1 package baby spinach,
   6-oz.)
1/4 cup water
1 package bacon slices (12-oz.), cut in half
1 Tablespoon American parsley, chopped for garnish, (optional)
20 to 24 toothpicks

Put oysters in strainer and rinse with water; drain and set aside. Heat olive oil in pot and add garlic. When garlic is lightly browned, add spinach. Toss lightly and add water. Sauté until spinach is limp and turns a darker green. (Do not boil and overcook.) Drain and set aside to cool.

Lay 1/2 bacon strip on chopping board and add oyster (if too big, cut in half or thirds) and 1 to 2 teaspoons of spinach. Wrap with strip of bacon and fasten with toothpick. Lay in foil-lined baking pan with toothpick facing up.

Bake at 350°F for 30 to 45 minutes or until bacon browns. Transfer oysters onto serving tray. Sprinkle parsley on top of oysters to garnish, if desired, and serve warm.

Note: Fresh oysters may be found in the refrigerated section at the grocery.

Shrimp Lumpia

yield: 30 pieces

✳ ✳

**30 shrimp (31- to 40-count) about 1 pound, cleaned
and cut to lay flat
1 to 2 carrots, cut into 30 carrot sticks about the length of
the shrimp
1 package string beans (8-oz.), cut to length of shrimp
(30 pieces)
1 package bean sprouts (10-oz.)
30 square lumpia wrappers (frozen Menlo® Pastry Wrapper/
Balutan-NG-Lumpia), thawed
oil for deep-frying**

Carefully separate lumpia wrappers. Lay one shrimp, carrot stick, and string bean along one end of lumpia wrapper (about 2 inches from edge closest to you). Place a very small handful of bean sprouts over shrimp and vegetables. Fold end over shrimp and vegetables and roll once. Fold over sides and roll. Place end-down. Repeat until all are done. Fry in 1/2-inch hot oil on medium until brown and crisp. Drain on paper towels. Serve with Vietnamese Lumpia Sauce.

**Vietnamese Lumpia Sauce:
1/2 cup fish sauce (Nguyen Chat Nuoc Mam)
1/2 cup water
1/3 cup plus 1 Tablespoon sugar (adjust to taste)
5 cloves garlic, crushed with garlic press
3 Tablespoons lemon juice
Hawaiian chili pepper (optional)**

Combine fish sauce, water, sugar, garlic, and lemon juice. Cut and use 1/4 inch of pointed end of chili pepper to begin with (very hot). Remove seeds if any. Mix in chili pepper and remove. Ajust to your taste.

Crispy Gau Gee

yield: 48–60 pieces

* *

Filling:
1/2 pound ground pork
1/2 pound shrimp, deveined, coarsely chopped
1/4 cup water chestnuts, chopped
1/4 cup dry shiitake mushrooms, softened (stems removed) and chopped
1/4 cup green onions, chopped
1 egg

Seasoning:
1 Tablespoon cornstarch
1 Tablespoon oyster sauce
1 teaspoon sugar
1 teaspoon soy sauce
1/2 teaspoon salt
1/4 teaspoon pepper

Wrapper:
2 packages won ton pi (10-oz. each)

Mix all filling ingredients. Mix in seasoning. Place 1 generous teaspoonful filling in center of wrapper. Moisten edges of wrapper and fold wrapper in half to a rectangular shape. Press edges together to seal. Deep-fry in oil until golden brown. Drain on paper towels and serve with dipping sauce.

Dipping Sauce:
Local Style—Mix together 3 tablespoons Colman's® Mustard with 2 teaspoons water to make a paste. Add 1/4 teaspoon sesame oil and 4 tablespoons soy sauce. Mix thoroughly.

Stuffed Aburage with Somen

yield: 48 pieces

* *

**6 packages fully cooked and seasoned fried bean curd
(3.88-oz. each), 8 pieces per package, rectangle type
(e.g., Inari Sushi-No-Moto)**
1 package somen (8-oz.)
2 blocks kamaboko (6-oz. each), sliced into thin strips
8 ounces green ocean salad
**6 ounces Tropics® Oriental Dressing (half of 12-oz. bottle),
adjust to taste**

Prepare seasoned fried bean curd (aburage) according to package directions and set aside. Reserve juices.

Break somen noodles in half before cooking. Cook somen according to directions on package. Drain thoroughly; cool.

Mix together somen, kamaboko, green ocean salad, oriental dressing, and juice from aburage. Squeeze aburage gently to remove excess liquid and stuff mixture into aburage. Refrigerate.

Note: Very light and refreshing. Very easy to prepare and very popular at potlucks. Also tasty without the aburage and eaten as a salad.

Salads

Broccoli Salad

yield: 3–4 servings

* *

3 to 4 cups broccoli (raw or blanched), cut into
    bite-sized pieces
1 small carrot, shredded
1/4 cup Maui onion or red onion, chopped
1/4 cup raisins, plumped in water and drained
6 strips bacon, cooked crisp and crumbled (for garnish)

Dressing:
1/2 cup mayonnaise
1/8 cup sugar
2 Tablespoons apple cider vinegar

Combine broccoli, carrot, onions, and raisins; chill. Blend together dressing ingredients and chill. Just before serving, toss together broccoli mix and desired amount of dressing. Garnish with crumbled bacon.

Pasta Salad

yield: 16–18 servings

* *

1 pound pasta (e.g., Tricolor Fusilli Springs rotini),
   prepared according to package directions
2 to 3 bell peppers (green, red, or yellow), chopped
2 to 3 tomatoes, cut
1 can small pitted olives (6-oz.), drained
1 cup red onion, chopped
1 can kidney beans (15.5-oz.), drained
1/4 cup dried basil leaves (optional)
1 cup Italian dressing (e.g., Bernstein's® Italian Dressing);
   add more to taste
salt and pepper to taste

Put cooked pasta in large bowl. Add chopped vegetables. Begin with 1 cup Italian dressing and add more to taste. Season with salt, pepper, and basil. Chill and serve.

Note: This is great for a potluck! Michelle Tobias prepared this tasty and colorful pasta salad for a baby shower luncheon, and we all enjoyed it.

Bean Salad

yield: 8–10 servings

* *

3 or more kinds of canned beans (green, yellow wax, kidney, soy, and garbanzo), drained well
1 medium Maui onion, thinly sliced
1 can whole mushrooms (6.5-oz.), drained
1 green pepper, sliced (optional)
1 can baby corn, whole spears (15-oz.) (optional)

Marinade:
1/4 cup sugar
2/3 cup vinegar
1/3 cup Wesson® oil
1 teaspoon salt

Marinate ingredients. Best if prepared a day or more before serving.

Note: Here is another "oldie but goodie" recipe from my Pūʻōhala Elementary School days in the 1970s. Thanks to Ethel Nishida who shared this recipe with us. I still make it, Ethel!

Broccoli Shrimp Salad

yield: 8–10 servings

* *

3 broccoli crowns (1-1/2 to 2 pounds), cut into
 bite-sized pieces and blanched
3/4 pound shrimp, cleaned and boiled
1/2 can whole olives (half of 6-oz. can), drained
2 jars marinated artichoke hearts (6.5-oz. each), drained
1 yellow bell pepper, diced into 1/2-inch squares
6 fresh mushrooms, quartered
6 cocktail tomatoes, cut in fourths, or 12 grape tomatoes,
 cut in half

Dressing:
Good Seasons® Italian packet (substitute with
 balsamic vinegar and olive oil)

Prepare dressing and set aside.

Place salad ingredients in large bowl. Refrigerate to chill.
Just before serving, gently toss all ingredients with desired
amount of dressing.

Variation: Artichokes may be cut into bite-sized pieces.
Cooked shrimp may also be cut into bite-sized pieces, if
necessary. Orange bell pepper may be added for more color.
Add more mushrooms and tomatoes, if desired.

*Note: Terry Arakaki, who taught with me at Kainalu
Elementary many years ago shared this great potluck salad
recipe that she had gotten from her friend Cindy Dela-Cruz.*

Chinese Chicken Salad

yield: 10–12 servings

* *

1 head iceberg lettuce, torn into bite-sized pieces
3 stalks celery, thinly sliced
1/4 cup green onion, chopped
2 to 3 romaine lettuce leaves, cut into bite-sized pieces (optional)
1 bunch Chinese parsley, chopped (optional)
1 package boiled ham, 8 slices (6-oz.), cut into thin strips
2 to 3 chicken breasts, cooked in lightly salted water, shredded
20 sheets wun tun pi, cut into thin strips and deep-fried, or 1 can
    La Choy® Chow Mein Noodles

Dressing:
4 Tablespoons sugar
2 teaspoons salt
1 teaspoon pepper
1/2 cup Wesson® oil
6 Tablespoons vinegar
1/2 teaspoon sesame oil

Combine dressing ingredients. Place in jar and shake well.

Mix all vegetables and refrigerate. Just before serving, add ham
and chicken and toss. Pour desired amount of dressing over and
toss. Add desired amount of wun tun pi or noodles; toss lightly.

*Note: There are many wonderful Chinese Chicken Salad recipes,
but this is our favorite. It is simple with a light, refreshing
dressing. It tastes great at any potluck gathering.*

Pine Nut Salad

yield: 6–8 servings

* *

1 head romaine lettuce, cut into bite-sized pieces
1/2 cup green onions, chopped
1/4 cup pine nuts, roasted at 350°F for 5 minutes
6 fresh mushrooms, sliced
1 can sliced olives (2.25-oz.), drained
croutons (optional)

Dressing:
1/2 cup olive oil
1/4 teaspoon salt
2 teaspoons white wine vinegar
1 teaspoon Dijon mustard
1/4 cup Parmesan cheese
2 cloves garlic, crushed

Combine dressing ingredients; shake well. Just before serving pour dressing over salad and toss lightly.

Variation: Substitute slivered almonds for pine nuts (not necessary to roast almonds).

Note: This salad with the great-tasting dressing was first shared by Sharon Smith at an 'Aikahi Elementary potluck many years ago. Since then it's been a favorite of mine. Everyone asks for this recipe as soon as they taste it.

Soba Salad

yield: 10–12 servings

* *

1 package buckwheat noodles (yamaimo soba 8.75-oz.), e.g.,
    Ishiguro brand
1/2 pound ocean salad
1/2 Maui onion or sweet onion, thinly sliced
1/2 pound imitation crab, shredded
1 package baby spinach leaves (6-oz.) or 1 bunch spinach
1 tomato, thinly sliced

Break soba noodles in half before cooking. Cook soba as
directed on package. Drain well. Place soba on large platter
or in 9×5×13 pan. Top with ocean salad, sliced onions,
imitation crab, spinach, and tomatoes in that order.

Dressing:
1/2 cup sugar
1/2 to 1 teaspoon black pepper
2 teaspoons salt
1/3 cup Japanese vinegar
1/2 cup or less vegetable oil
1 Tablespoon sesame oil
2 to 3 teaspoons lemon juice (about 1/2 lemon)

Mix well until sugar is dissolved. Pour over salad before
serving.

Variation: Substitute spinach with chopped watercress.

*Note: On one of my trips to Hilo, my cousin Miye Watanabe
introduced me to this very popular soba salad doing the
rounds. It's a great potluck salad. The dressing is especially
delicious!*

Spinach Salad
with Hot Dressing

yield: 4 servings

* *

1 bunch spinach, stems removed
1 cup fresh mushrooms (about 4 to 5 mushrooms), sliced
4 stalks green onions, thinly sliced
1 to 2 hard-boiled eggs, diced (for garnish)

Combine spinach, mushrooms, and green onions. Set aside diced eggs for garnish.

Dressing:
6 slices bacon
1/4 cup vinegar
2 Tablespoons water
1/2 teaspoon salt
1/4 teaspoon pepper (or less)
1/4 teaspoon dry mustard

Fry bacon until brown; drain and dice. Set aside. Drain bacon fat from frying pan; add vinegar, water, salt, pepper, and mustard. Blend well. Bring to a boil for 1 to 2 minutes. Mix in diced bacon.

Pour hot dressing over salad and toss lightly. Sprinkle diced egg over salad. Serve immediately.

Variation: Substitute 1/4 cup round onion, thinly slivered, for green onions. Add sliced olives as garnish.

Strawberry Salad

yield: 4–6 servings

* *

1 bunch spinach, torn into bite-sized pieces
2 cups fresh strawberries, chopped
1/2 cup pecans, chopped
2 Tablespoons butter

Dressing:
1/4 cup red onion, thinly sliced
1 cup oil
1/3 cup red wine vinegar
1/2 teaspoon salt
1/2 cup sugar
1 teaspoon dry mustard
1 teaspoon poppy seeds

Mix dressing ingredients and set aside. Melt butter and mix in chopped pecans. Toast buttered pecans in 350°F oven for 10 minutes. Toss together with spinach and strawberries. Pour dressing over spinach mixture.

Note: A surprisingly tasty combination, this salad has caught on in recent years. It is quite popular now.

Taegu Ocean Salad Linguine

yield: 10–12 servings

* *

1 package linguine (8-oz.), broken into thirds and cooked
   according to package directions, drained and cooled
3 ounces taegu
2 Japanese cucumbers, seeded and sliced into 1-inch strips
8 ounces imitation crab, shredded
8 ounces fresh green ocean salad
1/2 bottle furikake (half of 1.9-oz.), adjust to taste (i.e. aji nori
   furikake or nori komi furikake)
Tropics® Oriental Dressing (12-oz.), adjust to taste
Chinese parsley for garnish, (optional)

Mix cooked linguine with taegu, cucumbers, imitation crab, and ocean salad. Just before serving, mix in desired amount of Tropics® Oriental Dressing to taste. Garnish with Chinese parsley, if desired.

Note: This recipe originated from Linda Shimamoto via Ruby Saito to me. This is a very popular potluck dish with locals.

Tofu Salad

yield: 10 servings

* *

1 block firm tofu (20-oz.), cubed
1/2 Maui onion, thinly sliced
1 can salmon (7.5-oz.) or 1 can tuna (6-oz.)
1 package bean sprouts (10-oz.), parboiled, drained, and
    cooled (optional)
1 bunch watercress, cut into 1-1/2-inch pieces
1 to 2 tomatoes, cubed

Layer all the above in order listed in large salad bowl or platter, starting with tofu on the bottom. Place in refrigerator until ready to serve.

Dressing:
1/4 cup vegetable oil
1 Tablespoon sesame oil
1 clove garlic
1/2 cup soy sauce

Heat vegetable oil, sesame oil, and garlic until garlic is browned. Remove from heat and cool. Add soy sauce to cooled oil. Pour over salad just before serving.

Note: My nephew Henry Watanabe often requests Grandma Watanabe to prepare this salad for him. To me, this dressing is the best of all the tofu salad dressings out there.

Potato and Macaroni Salad

yield: 8–10 servings

* *

2 cups elbow macaroni
2 to 3 russet potatoes, boiled, peeled, and cut into cubes
3 to 4 eggs, hard-boiled and chopped
1 Tablespoon onion, finely diced
1 stalk celery, diced
1 Tablespoon sweet pickle relish
1 package imitation crab (8-oz.), shredded
1 cup frozen peas, parboiled
Mayonnaise to moisten ingredients
Salt and pepper to taste

Cook macaroni according to package directions. Rinse and drain thoroughly. Turn macaroni over occasionally until macaroni looks dry (about 30 minutes). In small bowl, combine onion, celery, and sweet pickle relish; set aside.

When items are cooled, combine all ingredients in large mixing bowl. Drain excess liquid from onion, celery, and pickle mixture before using. Mix all ingredients together to desired mayonnaise consistency; refrigerate.

Note: I overcook the potatoes so they are on the softer side and if some of the cubes fall apart and become like mashed potatoes, even better. That adds a binding consistency to the potato salad that makes the salad very tasty! This is a great local potato salad!

24-Hour Lettuce Salad

yield: 8–10 servings

* *

1 head iceberg lettuce, sliced
1 cucumber, sliced
1/4 cup celery, thinly sliced
1 can water chestnuts (8-oz.), sliced
1 package frozen peas (10-oz.), *do not thaw*
2 cups mayonnaise

Place lettuce in salad bowl. Add cucumbers, celery, water chestnuts, and frozen peas in that order. Spread mayonnaise over vegetables like frosting.

1/2 cup Parmesan cheese, grated
2 teaspoons sugar
1 teaspoon salt (or seasoned salt)
1/4 teaspoon garlic salt
bacon bits for garnish
2 tomatoes, sliced
6 hard-boiled eggs, sliced

Mix together Parmesan cheese, sugar, salt, and garlic salt and sprinkle over mayonnaise. Cover and refrigerate overnight. Before serving, garnish with bacon bits, sliced tomatoes, and eggs.

Sides

Baked Beans

yield: 8–10 servings

* *

4 slices bacon, chopped
1 onion, chopped
1 small Portuguese sausage (5-oz.), sliced
1 can pork and beans (15-oz.)
1 can kidney beans (15-oz.), drained
1 can pinto beans (15-oz.), drained
1/2 cup brown sugar, or less, as desired
1/3 cup catsup
2 teaspoons Worcestershire® sauce
1/4 cup mild cheddar cheese, grated
Parmesan cheese for sprinkling

Fry bacon until lightly browned. Add onion and Portuguese sausage and cook together until onion is tender. In large bowl, mix together all ingredients (except for the cheese) and place in greased casserole dish. Top with cheddar and Parmesan cheese. Bake at 350°F for 1 hour.

Scalloped Potatoes

yield: 12–14 servings

* *

5 to 6 medium potatoes, peeled and thinly sliced
salt and pepper to taste
1 onion, sliced
1 Portuguese sausage, mild or hot (10-oz.), or ham slices
1 can cream of mushroom soup (10.75-oz.)
1 can water (use soup can)

Layer potato slices in greased casserole, sprinkling each layer with salt and pepper and placing onion and meat of choice between layers of potato. Blend soup with water; pour over potato layers. Cover and bake at 350°F for 45 minutes. Uncover and bake for 45 minutes longer or until potatoes are tender and brown.

Choi Sum

yield: 3–4 servings

* *

1 bunch choi sum (about 3/4 pound)
1 Tablespoon oil
2 cloves garlic, crushed
pinch Hawaiian salt
1/2 cup water
1 Tablespoon oyster sauce (optional)

Wash choi sum and cut into 3-inch lengths. Heat skillet on medium-high, add oil and stir-fry garlic until lightly browned. Add choi sum; stir-fry until wilted and bright green in color. Sprinkle salt and add 1/2 cup water. Cover, lower heat, and simmer about 2 to 3 minutes or until choi sum is cooked tender, stirring occasionally. Mix in oyster sauce, if desired, or pour over choi sum in serving dish for stronger flavor.

Note: I don't remember ever eating choi sum until I married Don and became part of a Chinese family. My mother-in-law, Ellen Hee, showed me how to prepare many family recipes, and now choi sum is one of my favorite vegetable dishes! I also use this procedure for stir-frying watercress, mustard cabbage, and ong choy.

Green Bean Casserole

yield: 8 servings

* *

2 cans cut green beans (14.5-oz. each), drained
1 can Durkee® French fried onions (2.8-oz.), reserve 1/4 cup
1 can cream of mushroom soup (10.75-oz.)
dash pepper
1 can mushrooms, pieces and stems (6.5-oz.), with liquid
1/2 cup toasted slivered almonds (or less)
2/3 cup cheddar cheese, grated

Mix first 6 ingredients (minus the reserved 1/4 cup french-fried onions) together in bowl. Place in 2-quart casserole dish. Sprinkle the reserved 1/4 cup of french-fried onions. Then sprinkle the cheddar cheese over everything. Bake at 375°F for 30 minutes.

Note: This is traditional for Thanksgiving dinner. My daughter, Cheryl, adapted the original recipe that I gave her many years ago and her family loves it this way. Cheryl especially likes the crunchy texture of the added amount of toasted slivered almonds.

Kinpira Gobo
with Portuguese Sausage

yield: 4–5 servings

* *

1/2 pound gobo, scraped clean, slivered and soaked in water
1 Tablespoon oil
1 Tablespoon dried shrimp, minced
1/2 cup Portuguese sausage, cubed
1/4 cup soy sauce
3 Tablespoons sugar
1/8 teaspoon crushed red pepper
1/8 teaspoon cayenne pepper
dash pepper

Heat oil and sauté shrimp. Drain gobo and add to shrimp; stir-fry 1 minute. Add remaining ingredients and continue cooking over medium heat until sauce is absorbed.

Variation: Slivered carrots may be added for color.

Note: Very delicious! I tried several other recipes and found this kinpira most tasty of all. It's easy to prepare using simple ingredients.

Namul

yield: 6 servings

* *

1 package bean sprouts (10-oz.)
1 bunch watercress, cut into 2-inch lengths
water for boiling

Bring about 3 cups water to boil; mix in bean sprouts. After 1 minute, drain and rinse with cool water. Drain and squeeze excess water and place bean sprouts in bowl. Boil another 3 cups water. Put in watercress and cook about 2 to 3 minutes. Drain and rinse with cool water, then drain again thoroughly. Place in bowl with bean sprouts.

Sauce:
2 Tablespoons sesame seeds
1 teaspoon sugar
3 to 4 Tablespoons soy sauce
1 Tablespoon sesame oil
1 Tablespoon green onion
dash black pepper

Mix sauce ingredients. Pour over bean sprouts and watercress and lightly toss together.

Note: Dot Inoue, who is of Korean descent, was a great cook and seamstress. She handed down many of her recipes to her daughter, Evelyn, who is now sharing them with us.

Nishime

yield: 6–8 servings

* *

4 pieces chicken thighs, boneless and skinless
1 Tablespoon oil
2 cans chicken broth (14.5-oz. each)
4 pieces dried mushrooms, soaked and sliced
1 package nishime konbu (1-oz.)
1 container konyaku (10-oz.), cut into 3/4-inch × 1-inch pieces
1 can bamboo shoots (8.5-oz.), cut into 1-inch pieces
1/2 cup soy sauce
2/3 cup sugar (or less)
4 to 5 carrots, cut into 1-inch pieces
1 small daikon (about 1/2 pound), cut into 1-inch pieces
1 cup gobo
2 cups araimo, peeled and cut into 1-1/2-inch pieces
1 can lotus root (7-oz.) or 1/2 pound fresh lotus root
1 package aburage (2-oz.), cut into 1-1/2-inch pieces
1/4 pound Chinese peas, blanched

Wash konbu and tie into knots 1 inch apart. Cut between knots. Scrape burdock root clean and cut into 1/4-inch thick diagonal slices; soak in water until ready to use.

Cut chicken into bite-sized pieces. In large pot, fry chicken in oil until light brown. Add chicken broth, mushrooms, konbu, konyaku, and bamboo shoots. Cover and cook for 10 minutes. Add soy sauce and sugar, cover, and cook for 5 minutes. Add carrots, daikon, and gobo; cover and cook for 15 minutes. Add araimo, lotus root, and aburage. Cover and cook until araimo is fork-tender; toss gently occasionally. Garnish with Chinese peas.

Ong Choy and
Harm Ha (Shrimp Sauce)

yield: 4 servings

* *

1 bunch ong choy (about 1 pound), cut into 2-inch lengths
1 Tablespoon oil
1 clove garlic, crushed
pinch Hawaiian salt
1/2 cup water
1-1/2 teaspoon harm ha (adjust to taste)

Heat oil and sauté garlic. Add ong choy and cook about 3 minutes, stirring occasionally. Add a small pinch Hawaiian salt and water. Cover and simmer about 2 minutes. Add harm ha and continue cooking, uncovered, until ong choy is tender. Stir occasionally.

Note: This is another family favorite, which I learned to prepare from my mother-in-law, Ellen Hee, when I first got married. It is a tasty and nutritious vegetable dish. (It does have a distinct aroma, so you may wish to begin with less shrimp sauce.)

Cucumber Namasu

yield: 10–12 servings

* *

4 Japanese cucumbers, peeled
1 to 2 teaspoons salt (adjust to taste)
1/2 block kamaboko (half of 6-oz.), slivered
1/4 cup fueru wakame

Sauce:
1-1/4 cups sugar
1 cup Japanese vinegar
1 Tablespoon salt

Combine sauce ingredients; heat until sugar dissolves. Cool; set aside. (yield: 1-1/2 cups)

Cut peeled cucumbers into 1/2-inch-or-less round slices. (Use 2 shallow cuts then slice through.) Sprinkle salt over cucumbers, toss, and let sit about 30 to 40 minutes. Toss occasionally. (May add more salt if needed.) Drain. Do not squeeze. Let sit, draining, for a short while (about 15 minutes). Toss occasionally.

Soak wakame in water for 5 minutes or longer. May be soaked until ready to use. Drain and squeeze excess water.

Combine cucumber, kamaboko, and wakame. Pour about 1 cup sauce over and gently mix together. Reserve remaining sauce. Refrigerate overnight. Add more sauce the next day if needed.

Variation: Add slivered carrots or thinly sliced parboiled lotus root.

Note: For our New Year's party in Hilo, we always request cucumber namasu from my cousin Miye Watanabe. Miye shared this popular Hilo way of making namasu. Sometimes my mother squeezes in some fresh lemon juice for added flavor.

Takuan

yield: about 2 quarts

* *

4 to 5 pounds long daikon, cut into pieces of your choice
2-1/2 cups sugar
4 Tablespoons salt
4 Tablespoons Heinz® Vinegar
5 to 10 drops yellow food color (adjust to preference)

Combine sugar, salt, and vinegar; place over sliced daikon. Do not mix for 2 hours. Mix after 2 hours and leave for another hour. Add yellow food color; leave for 30 minutes. Place in clean jars and refrigerate.

Suggestion: Daikon may be cut thick or thin, in rounds, half-circles or lengthwise. For a little spicy flavor, add Hawaiian chili peppers to your taste.

Note: Dot Inoue recommended selecting young daikon, the ones that are usually small and slender. Daikon may be peeled or not peeled. Leaving the skin on gives it an extra crunch.

Roasted Vegetables

yield: 4 servings

* *

1 pound green beans (or asparagus, broccoli, squash, etc.)
Olive oil for coating vegetables
Salt and pepper to taste

Miso Dip Dressing:
1/2 cup mayonnaise
1/2 teaspoon sugar
4 teaspoons Japanese rice vinegar
1 Tablespoon white miso
1-1/2 Tablespoons peanut butter
1/2 teaspoon ginger, grated
1/2 teaspoon garlic, grated or pressed
2 teaspoons sesame oil
1 teaspoon roasted sesame seeds

Mix dressing ingredients in the order above. Refrigerate.

Toss vegetables with enough olive oil to lightly coat. Season with salt and pepper. Place on cookie sheet. Bake at 400°F to 450°F. Check after 10 minutes for doneness. Serve with Miso Dip Dressing.

Note: This recipe came to me highly recommended by Charlene Galapir while I was in Hilo. She got it from Ardis Ono who is encouraging healthy cooking. The Miso Dip Dressing also tastes great on fresh raw vegetables. This will certainly encourage more people to eat their vegetables!

Gon Lo Mein

yield: 10–12 servings

* *

2 pounds fried chow mein noodles
1/4 cup oyster sauce
1/4 cup sesame oil
oil for stir-frying
Hawaiian salt to season
1/4 pound char siu, slivered for garnish
Chinese parsley, for garnish

Vegetables:
1 small onion, slivered
2 stalks celery, julienned
1 small carrot, julienned
1/4 pound snow peas
1 package bean sprout mixture (12-oz.)
6 dried shiitake mushrooms, softened in water, sliced

Combine chow mein noodles with oyster sauce and sesame oil and marinate for 1 hour. In a heavy frying pan or wok, heat oil, and stir-fry noodles. Set aside.

Stir-fry lightly each vegetable separately in oil and Hawaiian salt (except mushroom). Set aside. Stir-fry mushroom without salt and return all ingredients (except char siu and Chinese parsley) to pan and toss together. Place on platter and garnish with char siu and Chinese parsley.

Note: Always a local favorite in any potluck gathering.

Soups

Mushroom Soup

yield: 6 servings

* *

4 cans chicken broth (14.5-oz. each)
3 Tablespoons soy sauce
3 cloves garlic, crushed
2 teaspoons grated fresh ginger
4 cups assorted mushrooms, sliced (e.g., white buttons,
    portobello, crimini, shiitake)
1 large carrot, sliced
1/4 head cabbage, cut in wedges
1 pound boneless, skinless chicken breasts or thighs,
    thinly sliced
2 cups fresh udon noodles (or substitute 2 cups cooked
    linguine)
1 to 2 stalks green onions, thinly sliced
2 cups spinach leaves, shredded
black pepper to taste
1 Tablespoon mirin (optional)

In large pot, combine chicken broth, soy sauce, garlic, ginger, mushrooms, carrot, and cabbage. Cover; bring to boil. Add chicken and simmer until mushrooms are soft, about 5 minutes. Stir in noodles, green onions, and spinach. Simmer 2 minutes more or until greens are wilted. Season with pepper and mirin to taste.

Hint: If using dried shiitake, soak in warm water until softened and discard stems. Portobello tends to make the soup a darker color so you may not want to include it.

Note: Eloise Yano recommended this healthy soup of mushrooms, which may help to boost immunity, fend off infections, and may have anti-cancer properties and other benefits. This soup is also tasty. Eloise says this is a good dish to give to those who are ill. She uses a package of ready-to-use udon noodles (7.22-oz.) (e.g., Myojo® brand found on most grocery shelves; do not use the soup seasoning packet, however).

Black Bean Soup

yield: 12–15 servings

* *

2 cans whole kernel corn (15-oz. each), drained
2 cans black beans (15-oz. each), drain only one can
1 can diced tomatoes with green chilies (14.5-oz. each)
2 cans chicken broth (14.5-oz. each)
2 cans chunk chicken in water (10-oz. each), or meat from
    1 roast chicken, chopped (about 3 cups)
black pepper to season

Combine all ingredients and bring to boil; simmer 5 minutes.

Note: This soup, a little on the spicy side, is quite popular with young adults. It is very tasty and so quick and easy to prepare. My young neighbor, Coreen Mijo, got this recipe from her friend Debbie Murata and shared it with me.

Watercress Egg-Drop Soup

yield: 4 servings

* *

2 cans chicken broth (14.5-oz. each)
1 clove garlic, lightly crushed
2 thin slices fresh ginger
1 bunch watercress, coarsely chopped into 1-1/2-inch lengths
1 egg, lightly beaten

Combine first 3 ingredients in medium saucepan; bring to boil. Add watercress and simmer until softened. Add egg, stirring until egg is lightly cooked. Remove garlic and ginger slices. Serve immediately.

Chinese Cabbage Soup

yield: 4–6 servings

* *

3 to 4 ounces lean pork, finely sliced

Marinade:
1 teaspoon cornstarch
2 teaspoons soy sauce
1/2 teaspoon sugar
1/4 teaspoon pepper

Combine above and marinate pork at least 15 minutes.

vegetable oil
2 to 3 thin slices ginger
1 teaspoon salt
6 cups boiling water
4 cups Chinese cabbage, coarsely sliced

Heat a little oil in pot, just enough to grease bottom of pot. Fry ginger and salt for 30 seconds. Pour in 6 cups of boiling water. Cover pot with lid and simmer for 8 minutes. Add seasoned pork; simmer for 10 minutes, skimming off residue. Remove ginger slices. Add Chinese cabbage; simmer another 5 minutes or until cabbage is cooked to your taste.

Note: Basic simple Chinese soup is generally made with lean pork marinated at least 15 minutes. When using soup bones of any type of meat, cover with water and cook at least 1-1/2 hours before adding seasoning and vegetables.

Country Comfort Corn Chowder

yield: 12–14 servings

* *

1/2 pound bacon, chopped
1 medium onion, chopped
1 to 2 stalks celery, chopped
1/4 to 1/2 cup flour
1 quart water (more if necessary)
4 to 5 medium potatoes, diced into chunks
2 cans cream-style corn (14.75-oz. each)
salt and pepper to taste
1 pint Half & Half
4 Tablespoons butter (optional)

Fry bacon until almost done. Add onion and celery; sauté until slightly browned. Gradually blend in flour. Mixture will be thick. Slowly add water and mix until smooth. Add potatoes and bring to a slow boil. Add more water if necessary. Reduce heat and simmer for about 15 to 20 minutes or until potatoes are cooked. Stir occasionally. Add corn and bring to simmer again. Season with salt and pepper and taste; adjust as necessary. Add the Half & Half and stir until mixed well. Just before serving, add butter, if desired, and stir until melted. Serve immediately.

Variations: Add 1 to 2 cans minced clams; diced shiitake mushrooms, soaked and sliced; diced carrots, etc., or top with seasoned croutons just before serving.

Note: Thanks to Devin Fujioka, who was an 11-year-old from Kamuela on the Big Island several years ago when he shared this family favorite in his school project cookbook. This corn chowder is so rich and delicious it was brought to my attention as the best! Lisa Fujioka, Devin's mother, created this for those chilly Kamuela nights and named it Country Comfort Corn Chowder.

Hearty Miso Soup

yield: 6 servings

* *

2 Tablespoons small iriko
4 cups water
1/2 cup round onion, chopped
1 potato, peeled, cut in half lengthwise, then cut into
    1/4-inch slices
1/4 block kamaboko, cut into strips
1 aburage, cut into strips
1 ounce somen (a small handful), soaked and cut into
    shorter lengths
4 to 5 Tablespoons miso, blended with a little water
1/4 cup green onion, chopped for garnish

Combine first three ingredients and simmer, covered, about 15 minutes. Add potato, kamaboko, aburage, and somen; simmer another 6 to 8 minutes. Stir in blended miso; simmer a minute and serve in individual bowls. Sprinkle green onion on top, if desired.

Note: I met my good friend Eleanor Tokunaga at the supermarket one day and asked her for her favorite soup recipe. I jotted down her recipe for her hearty miso soup which she calls "a meal in itself." She also substitutes udon noodles for the somen if she has some udon available. If she has gobo, she'll put that in, too.

Hot and Sour Soup

yield: 4 servings

* *

2 cans chicken broth (14.5-oz. each) or 4 cups chicken broth
1/4 cup lean pork or chicken, cut into strips
2 Tablespoons bamboo shoots, julienned
1 Tablespoon black fungus, softened in water and julienned
2 Tablespoons soy sauce
1/2 teaspoon pepper (or less, adjust to taste)
3 Tablespoons cornstarch blended with 3 Tablespoons water
2 eggs, lightly beaten
2 Tablespoons vinegar
1 teaspoon sesame oil
2 teaspoons green onions, thinly sliced

Heat chicken broth; add pork or chicken, bamboo shoots, and black fungus. Bring to boil; add soy sauce and pepper. Lower heat and simmer 2 to 3 minutes. While soup is simmering, stir in cornstarch and water mixture, making certain that it is mixed evenly. Stir eggs and vinegar into soup in a steady stream; simmer 1 to 2 minutes. Add sesame oil and green onions just before serving.

Note: Very quick and simple to prepare and very tasty. I lessened the amount of pepper, but that's a matter of preference.

Jook (Chinese Rice Porridge)

yield: 6–8 servings

* *

chicken or turkey bones
1 cup uncooked rice
1 teaspoon salt
1/2 teaspoon sherry
1/2 teaspoon oil
2 Tablespoons chung choi, rinsed and minced

Condiments:
iceberg lettuce leaves, shredded
green onions, thinly sliced
soy sauce and pepper to taste
Chinese parsley, chopped (optional)
"1,000-year-old" eggs, chopped (optional)
fried won ton pi strips (optional)

In large pot, place chicken or turkey bones and cover with water; bring to boil and simmer about 1 to 1-1/2 hours. Cool and strain broth to remove bones. Shred any meat off bones; set aside. Add enough water to broth to measure 11 cups liquid and pour back into pot.

Rinse rice until water is clear. Cover rice with warm water and stir in salt, sherry, and oil. Let sit for 15 minutes.

Bring broth to boil and add rice with liquid, chung choi, and any shredded meat. Simmer about 1 hour at somewhere between medium and medium-low heat with cover slightly ajar. Stir occasionally and adjust heat as necessary. Add more water if needed. (Be careful of jook spilling over or sticking to pot.)

Serve jook in bowls and provide condiments for garnish. Provide soy sauce and pepper also.

Note: My husband, Don, likes chicken liver in jook. I boil chicken livers separately and cut into slices. Just before serving, I add a portion serving of liver into the jook for him, heat, and serve.

Imitation Bird Nest Soup

yield: 5–6 servings

* *

1 bundle long rice (2-oz.), soaked in hot water for 1 hour
4 shiitake mushrooms, soaked in water to soften
1 cup bamboo shoots, thinly sliced
3 cans chicken broth (14.5-oz. each)
1/2 cup pork, thinly sliced
1/2 cup ham, thinly sliced
2 eggs, beaten
1/2 cup green onions, thinly sliced

Drain long rice and cut into approximately 1/4-inch pieces. Drain mushrooms; discard stems and slice mushrooms into thin strips. Combine long rice, mushrooms, bamboo shoots, and broth; bring to boil. Add pork and ham; simmer for 15 to 20 minutes. Just before serving, stir in beaten eggs and green onions.

Variation: Substitute green onions with Chinese parsley. Substitute bamboo shoots with 1/2 cup chopped water chestnuts.

Minestrone Soup

yield: 12–14 servings

* *

1 can condensed beef consommé (10.5-oz.)
2 teaspoons instant beef bouillon or 2 bouillon cubes
5 cups water
1 large onion, finely chopped
1 clove garlic, minced
3 Tablespoons fresh parsley, chopped, or 1 Tablespoon dry
2 carrots, shredded or finely chopped
2 stalks celery with leaves, diced
1 large potato, diced
1-1/4 teaspoons Italian seasoning

Combine all ingredients above; boil 1 minute. Lower heat, cover, and simmer 30 minutes, stirring occasionally.

1 pound ground beef, cooked and drained
1 cup macaroni, uncooked
1 can tomatoes with liquid (28-oz.), do not drain, but chop
    tomatoes into smaller pieces
1 teaspoon salt
1/4 teaspoon pepper
1 can kidney beans (15-oz.), with liquid

Add remaining ingredients and simmer additional 20 minutes.

Optional: Serve with a sprinkle of Parmesan cheese, if desired.

Note: Mary Alice Clark gave me this fantastic Minestrone Soup recipe. It's easier to make than it appears and it's so-o-o good. Many others enjoyed it so much that Mary Alice used to make this soup as a Christmas gift to her friends and neighbors.

Oxtail Soup

yield: 4 – 6 servings

* *

4 pounds oxtail, cut into pieces
2 cubes beef bouillon (Knorr® brand, Extra Large Cubes)
2 cubes chicken bouillon (Knorr® brand, Extra Large Cubes)
5 whole star anise
4 slivers ginger
1 cup raw peanuts, shelled and skinned
Hawaiian salt to taste
Chinese parsley for garnish

Parboil oxtail 20 to 30 minutes. Rinse and trim fat. Place in pot and cover with water approximately 2 inches above oxtail. Bring to boil and add bouillon cubes, star anise, and ginger. Simmer for 1 hour. Add peanuts. Simmer for another 1 to 1-1/2 hours, or until oxtail is tender. Skim residue from broth. Add Hawaiian salt to taste. Garnish with Chinese parsley.

Variation: Serve with ground ginger and soy sauce as a condiment. Serve with cooked vegetables such as mustard cabbage and Chinese cabbage that can be added to soup if desired.

Hint: Soak raw shelled peanuts in warm water to easily remove skin.

Portuguese Bean Soup

yield: 8–10 servings

* *

1 to 2 pounds ham shank (or ham hock)
3 cans chicken broth (14.5-oz. each)
2 cans kidney beans (15-oz. each)
2 cans tomato sauce (8-oz. each)
1 clove garlic, crushed
1 teaspoon pepper or less
1 medium onion, chopped
4 potatoes, cubed into 1-1/2-inch pieces
4 carrots, cut into 1-1/2-inch pieces
1 Portuguese sausage (10-oz.), cut into 1/2-inch slices
1 bay leaf
1 small head cabbage

In very large pot, cover ham shank with chicken broth. Add enough water to cover and boil until tender (about 2 hours). Skim off fat while cooking. Add rest of ingredients* and cook until tender. Continue to skim off fat.

*Add potatoes 15 minutes after carrots.

Note: This is my all-time favorite Portuguese Bean Soup. It is so delicious! You can prepare this a day or two ahead and just heat it up for a quick meal.

Seafood Bisque

yield: 4–6 servings

* *

2 Tablespoons butter
2 cloves garlic, minced
3 stalks celery, minced
2 cans cream of celery soup (10.7-oz. each)
5 cans water (use soup can)
1 pound fish, cut in 1-inch pieces (e.g., mahimahi and cod)
12 clams in shell, rinsed
1/2 pound shrimp, shell on (51- to 60-count)
1 Tablespoon parsley, chopped (or parsley flakes)
salt and pepper to taste

Melt butter in large pot; add garlic and celery and sauté. Add cream of celery soup and water. Bring to boil. Add fish; cook for 5 minutes. Lower heat; add clams and shrimp. Cover and simmer for 10 to 15 minutes. Add parsley. Season with salt and pepper.

Note: Tastes great with garlic bread. Scallops and crab may be substituted.

Turkey Chowder

yield: 2–3 servings

* *

1 strip bacon, chopped
1/4 cup onion, diced
2 stalks celery, diced
1 large potato, cubed
1 cup cooked turkey, diced
2 cups turkey broth or 1 can chicken broth (14.5-oz.)
1 can whole kernel corn (11-oz.)
2 Tablespoons fresh parsley, chopped
2 Tablespoons flour
1 cup milk
salt and pepper to taste

In medium saucepan, fry bacon pieces until crispy; drain, reserving about 2 tablespoons bacon drippings. Add onion and celery to bacon and drippings. Cook until soft. Add broth (if using 1 can chicken broth, add enough water to make 2 cups). Heat to boiling and add potatoes and turkey. Simmer until potatoes are tender. Add corn and parsley. Blend flour with milk and stir into cooking mixture. Cook about 15 minutes longer, stirring occasionally.

Note: It's a great way to use leftover turkey after Thanksgiving.

Kim Chee Soup

yield: 4 servings

* *

8 to 10 ounces ground pork or thinly sliced lean pork*
3 slices fresh ginger
3 cans chicken broth (14.5-oz. each)
1 jar kim chee (12-oz., e.g., Kohala Won-Bok® Kim Chee),
**   include liquid**
1-1/2 pounds wintermelon or long squash, cut into
**   1-1/2 × 2-1/2-inch pieces (about 15)**
1 block firm tofu (20-oz.), cut into 1-inch cubes

Brown ground pork with ginger; drain oil. Add chicken broth.
Chop kim chee into smaller pieces and, together with kim chee
liquid, add to soup. Add wintermelon or long squash and simmer for 15 to 20 minutes or until wintermelon or long squash
becomes soft. Add tofu and cook about 1 to 2 minutes more.

*Marinate thinly sliced lean pork about 15 minutes with:

    1 teaspoon cornstarch

    2 teaspoons or more soy sauce

    1/2 teaspoon sugar

    1/4 teaspoon pepper

Brown marinated pork with ginger in little oil before adding
chicken broth.

Optional: Lessen amount if kim chee is too hot for your
taste.

Won Ton Soup

yield: 5 – 6 servings

* *

3 packages won ton pi wrappers (12-oz. each), or 1 pound
4 cans chicken broth (14.5-oz. each)
Chinese parsley or green onions, chopped,
for garnish (optional)
3 quarts water

Filling:
1 pound ground pork
1/2 pound shrimp, cleaned and chopped
1/2 cup water chestnuts, finely minced
1 teaspoon Hawaiian salt
1 teaspoon sesame oil
1 teaspoon soy sauce
1/2 teaspoon cornstarch
1/2 teaspoon sugar
1/2 teaspoon oyster sauce

Combine filling ingredients and mix well. Place about 1 teaspoon of pork filling on won ton pi wrapper. Wet edges and fold into a triangle. Wet left side of won ton pi skin. Pull sides back and pinch together, placing one side on top of the sealer.

Boil 3 quarts water rapidly. Place 10 won tons into boiling water. Won tons are cooked when they float to the top. Test for doneness. More filling may require more cooking time. Repeat procedure until all are cooked. Rinse in cold water as they are removed. Drain and place in soup bowls. Pour desired amount of heated chicken broth over won tons. Garnish with Chinese parsley or green onions, if desired.

Main Dishes

Beef Broccoli

yield: 4 servings

* *

1 pound meat, sliced
2 teaspoons sugar
2 Tablespoons soy sauce
1 Tablespoon ginger, crushed
2 Tablespoons sherry or whiskey
2 Tablespoons flour
2 pounds broccoli, sliced
1/2 teaspoon salt
1/2 cup water
oil for frying

Marinate meat with sugar, soy sauce, ginger, sherry, and flour. Set aside. Heat 1 teaspoon oil and stir-fry broccoli. Add salt and water. Simmer, covered, until tender and take out. (Do not overcook broccoli.) In the same pan, heat 1 tablespoon oil and stir-fry meat for 2 minutes. Add broccoli and mix together until heated through.

Beef Tomato

yield: 4–6 servings

* *

1 pound beef (sirloin, flank, sirloin tip, round, etc.),
    thinly sliced
1 onion, wedged
2 stalks celery, cut diagonally in thick slices
2 green peppers, wedged
pinch of salt
1 to 2 tomatoes, wedged
2 stalks green onion, cut in 1-1/2-inch lengths
oil for frying

Marinade:
1-inch piece fresh ginger, crushed
1 clove garlic, crushed
1/2 teaspoon sugar
1/2 teaspoon salt
2 Tablespoons soy sauce
1 Tablespoon sherry
pinch of pepper
1 Tablespoon cornstarch
1 Tablespoon oil

Gravy:
1 Tablespoon cornstarch
1-1/2 teaspoons sugar
1 teaspoon soy sauce
1/2 teaspoon Worcestershire® sauce
1 Tablespoon catsup (or more to your taste)

Soak beef slices in marinade for 15 to 20 minutes. Heat 2 teaspoons oil in pan or wok and stir-fry round onion, celery, and bell pepper on medium-high heat for about 2 minutes. Season with salt to your taste. Add tomatoes and cook an additional minute. Remove from pan. Heat 2 teaspoons oil in the same pan and sauté beef until medium rare. Remove garlic and ginger. Add the stir-fried vegetables, green onion, and gravy. Bring to a quick boil; turn heat off.

Corned Beef Hash Patties

yield: 4–6 servings

* *

1 can corned beef
3 to 4 medium potatoes
1/4 cup minced onions
3 eggs, beaten
salt and pepper to season
Chinese parsley, minced (optional)
flour for dredging
oil for frying

Cut potatoes in half; boil in enough water until soft. Peel skin and mash in bowl. Add corned beef, onions, eggs, and seasoning. Mix together. Form into patties; dredge in flour. Heat pan on medium heat; add about 1 to 2 tablespoons oil. Fry patties, adding oil as needed.

Note: This is my Aunty Fusako Martinez's recipe; whenever she makes this for potluck, nothing is left!

Jumbo's Restaurant's Beef Stew

yield: 6–8 servings

* *

3 to 4 pounds stew meat, cut into 1-1/2-inch cubes
salt and pepper to season
4 cloves garlic, crushed
1 Tablespoon oil
1/2 cup red wine
1 large onion, cut in chunks
5 stalks celery, cut in 1/2-inch slices
2 Tablespoons sugar
2 Tablespoons salt
1 teaspoon black pepper
2 bay leaves
1 can Hunt's® tomato paste (6-oz.)
4 carrots, cut into large pieces
3 to 4 potatoes, cut into large pieces
6 Tablespoons cornstarch mixed with 6 Tablespoons water

Heat oil and braise stew meat on medium-high heat for approximately 5 minutes, or until brown. (Lightly salt and pepper meat while cooking.) Add garlic and sauté a few minutes to release the flavor. Add wine and sauté for another 3 to 5 minutes, or until alcohol is evaporated. Add onions and celery and cook for a few minutes.

Cover the meat with water (about 12 cups water). Add spices, bay leaves, and tomato paste; bring to boil. Lower heat to medium-low, cover, and cook for approximately 1 hour, or until meat is tender. Add carrots and cook for approximately 10 minutes. Add potatoes, continue cooking until vegetables are tender. Thicken with cornstarch mixture to desired consistency and simmer for a few minutes.

Note: This is a reduced version of Jumbo's Restaurant's award-winning famous beef stew. Jumbo's made this and their fried min the favorites of local folks. Jumbo's is just a memory now, but their beef stew is still great!

Sukiyaki

yield: 4 servings

* *

1 pound beef or deboned chicken breasts, thinly sliced
1 Tablespoon oil
1/3 cup sugar
1/2 cup soy sauce
1/4 cup beer or sherry
1 onion, thinly sliced
1/2 cup chicken broth
1 can Sukiyaki No Tomo (8.75-oz.), slice contents if needed
1/2 block firm tofu, cubed (half of 20-oz. container)
1 bunch long rice, softened in water and cut in 2-inch
**   lengths (2-oz.)**
2 cups watercress, cut in 1-1/2-inch pieces
1 to 2 stalks green onions, cut in 1-1/2-inch pieces

Heat oil in skillet. Brown beef or chicken. Add sugar, soy sauce, and beer; simmer for a few minutes. Add onion and cook until tender. Add all other ingredients (except green vegetables). Cook 2 to 3 minutes. (Add more chicken broth if necessary.) Add green vegetables; cook until watercress is soft and tender.

Stuffed Cabbage Rolls

yield: 6 servings

* *

1/2 pound ground beef
1/2 pound ground pork
3/4 cup cooked rice
1 egg, beaten
1/2 cup milk
1/4 cup onion, finely chopped
1 teaspoon Worcestershire® sauce
3/4 teaspoon salt
dash of pepper
3 quarts water
12 cabbage leaves

Sauce:
1 can tomato soup (10.75-oz.)
1 Tablespoon brown sugar
1 Tablespoon lemon juice

In a bowl, combine pork, ground beef, rice, egg, milk, onion, Worcestershire® sauce, salt, and pepper; mix well. Boil 3 quarts water and immerse cabbage leaves about 3 minutes, or until limp; drain. Place about 1/4 cup meat mixture on each leaf; fold in sides. Starting at unfolded edge, roll up each leaf, making sure folded sides are included in roll. Arrange in foil-lined 9 × 13 baking dish.

Stir together sauce ingredients; pour over cabbage rolls. Bake, uncovered at 350°F for 1 hour and 15 minutes, basting once or twice with sauce.

Easy Pot Roast

yield: 6–8 servings

* *

3 to 4 pounds 7-bone chuck roast
salt and pepper to season
2 Tablespoons oil
1 clove garlic, crushed
3 carrots, cut in 3-inch pieces
2 potatoes, quartered
2 onions, halved
1 can cream of mushroom soup (10.75-oz.)
1 envelope onion soup mix

Cut roast into 6 to 8 pieces (include bone in); season with salt and pepper. In large skillet, heat oil and brown garlic. Add roast pieces and brown on all sides. Lower heat. Spread cream of mushroom soup over roast pieces; sprinkle onion soup mix over that. Place carrots, potatoes, and onions in the skillet. Cover and cook on low heat about 45 to 60 minutes, or until roast and vegetables are fork tender.

Note: This recipe was often requested by the grandchildren to Grandma Watanabe when they had dinner together.

Pasta Salad (Page 21)

Lemon Bars (Page 142)

Tri-Colored Mochi (Page 150)

Broccoli Shrimp Salad (Page 23)

Chicken Katsu (Page 88)

Moist Banana Cake (Page 126)   Pumpkin Custard Pie (Page 134)
and Tofu Pie (Page 133)

Stuffed Aburage with Somen (Page 18)

Blueberry Mochi (Page 147)

Buffalo Wings (Page 10)

Furikake Seared 'Ahi (Page 13)

Beef Tomato (Page 63)

Oyster Bacon Wrap (Page 15)   Strawberry Salad (Page 28)

Okinawan Sweet Potato Pie with Haupia Topping (Page 131)

Nishime (Page 39)

'Ahi Limu Poke (Page 2) and Mochiko Chicken (Page 96)

Blueberry Cream Cheese Pie (Page 137)

Bacardi® Rum Cake (Page 114)

Lasagna
yield: 8–10 servings

* *

2 pounds hamburger
1 Tablespoon oil
1 clove garlic, minced
1 round onion, chopped
1 green pepper, chopped
1 can tomato sauce (15-oz.)
1 can tomato sauce (8-oz.)
2 teaspoons salt
2 cans (6-oz. each) "basil, garlic, & oregano" tomato paste
3 cans water (measure with tomato paste can)
2 envelopes spaghetti sauce mix (1.37-oz. each)
1 box extra-wide lasagna noodles (16-oz.)
1 package mozzarella cheese slices (6-oz.)

Heat oil, brown garlic slightly. Add onion and green pepper and cook until tender. Add meat; do not overcook the meat. Add rest of ingredients (except noodles and mozzarella cheese slices) and simmer about 1 hour.

Cook noodles according to package directions. Rinse with cold water; drain.

Alternate layers of noodles and meat mixture in a 10×14 roasting pan, ending with meat mixture. Top with mozzarella cheese sheets. Bake at 325°F, uncovered, approximately 30 to 45 minutes or until cheese is lightly browned.

Optional: Add 1 container (16-oz.) cottage cheese, small curd, to layers.

Note: I sometimes use 2 Pyrex® 7-1/2 × 11-3/4 pans. I can share one pan with relatives. My niece Pat especially enjoyed this lasagna, requesting no cottage cheese.

No-Fail Roast Beef

yield: 4–6 servings

* *

any size rib roast beef

Salt and pepper roast and let stand at room temperature for 1 hour. (**Optional:** poke holes here and there in the roast and put in little pieces of garlic.) Place beef, fat side up, in open roaster (not covered) and put in 350°F oven for 1 hour. Turn off heat but DO NOT OPEN DOOR AT ANY TIME UNTIL READY TO SERVE.

For rare beef: 45 minutes before serving, turn oven to 300°F.

For medium beef: 50 minutes before serving, turn oven to 300°F.

For medium-well done beef: 55 minutes before serving, turn oven to 300°F.

Note: Roast can be started in midafternoon or earlier. Allow at least 3 hours in the oven to complete cooking. Thanks to Janet Hirota and Ethel Nishida who shared this wonderful secret with the Pūʻōhala Elementary faculty and staff in 1975. It really is a no-fail recipe! I've been using it ever since.

DeLuz Vindha D'Ahlos Roast

yield: 3–4 servings

* *

2 to 3 pounds roast (chuck or crossrib roast)
1 chili pepper*
4 to 5 cloves garlic, crushed
1-1/2 Tablespoons Hawaiian salt
1/2 cup apple cider vinegar
1/2 cup water
2 potatoes, cut into large chunks
3 carrots, cut into large chunks
1 Portuguese sausage (5-oz.), sliced diagonally in
   1-1/2-inch lengths

Slice pepper lengthwise in three pieces. Mix pepper, garlic, salt, and vinegar until salt dissolves. Rub on roast and marinate overnight in the refrigerator. Turn roast over a couple of times. When ready to cook, place roast with marinade liquid in a roasting pan. Add water, vegetables, and sausage. Cover with foil and bake at 300°F for 2 hours. Uncover and bake for an additional 30 minutes or until done.

*Habanero, hottest; serrano, hotter than jalapeño; and jalapeño, hot and spicy.

Note: The general rule is 1 hour roasting time per pound at 300°F. If roast is more or less than 3 pounds, adjust roasting time. This is a scaled-down version of Jackie DeLuz Watanabe's original recipe to accomodate smaller families. My neighbor, Darleen Dyer, has fond memories of her grandmother preparing vindha d'ahlos and liked this recipe.

Roast Lamb

yield: 6–8 servings

* *

5 pounds boned rolled leg of lamb
salt and pepper to season
3 cloves garlic
2 cans mushrooms (4-oz.), pieces and stems with liquid
2 to 3 round onions, chopped

Remove netting around rolled leg of lamb; unroll lamb. Prepare roast by rubbing salt and pepper all over. Slice garlic into slivers and poke into small gashes in surface of lamb. Fold over lamb and place, skin side up, in a foil-lined roasting pan. Roast, uncovered, at 325°F about 25 minutes per pound (or internal temperature of 165°F).

About 1 hour before roast is done, add onions and mushrooms. Continue roasting, basting with onion-mushroom sauce. Let roast set for 20 minutes before slicing. Serve with onion-mushroom sauce.

Optional: To make gravy, scoop out all onions and mushrooms. Make gravy with drippings, using cornstarch and chicken broth to thicken.

Note: I got this recipe from Jean Tanimoto, a former teacher at Pūʻōhala Elementary School and a super cook! I love this roast lamb. Although retired, she is still preparing her delicious treats for the Pūʻōhala staff.

Lazy-Style Laulau

yield: 10–12 servings

* *

8 ti leaves, rinsed and stiff rib removed
4 pounds taro (lū'au) leaves, rinsed and stems removed
3 pounds pork butt, cut into 1 × 1-inch chunks
1 to 2 pounds salted butterfish, cut into bite-sized pieces
2 Tablespoons Hawaiian salt
1 cup water

Line a large roasting pan with foil. Lay 4 ti leaves in the pan, overlapping one over another. Use half of the lū'au leaves over the ti leaves. Arrange pork and fish evenly on leaves. Sprinkle with salt. Place remaining lū'au leaves on top. Pour water over all and cover with ti leaves on top. Cover pan tightly with foil. Bake at 350°F for 3 hours.

Variation: Sweet potatoes may be added before covering with ti leaves.

*Tonkatsu

yield: 5 servings

* *

5 pork cutlets
oil for browning
salt, pepper, and garlic salt to season
1/2 cup flour for coating
1/2 cup bread crumbs
1 egg, beaten

Sauce:
1/2 cup catsup
1 teaspoon dry mustard
1 Tablespoon water
2 Tablespoons Worcestershire® sauce
1/2 teaspoon Tabasco® sauce

Pound pork cutlets and season with salt, pepper, and garlic salt. Let set for 15 minutes. Dredge pork cutlets in flour, dip in egg, and roll in bread crumbs. Heat oil and cook until golden brown. Drain on paper towel. Slice into 1-inch strips. Combine sauce and serve with cutlets.

Sari Sari

yield: 4 – 5 servings

* *

1/2 pound Chinese roast pork
1 Tablespoon oil
3 cloves garlic, crushed
1/2 round onion, wedged
1 tomato, wedged
1 teaspoon salt, or to taste
1 cup water or chicken broth
2 long-type eggplants, halved lengthwise and cut in
    1-inch slices
1/2 pound string beans, cut into thirds
1 long squash, peeled, cut into chunks (or 1/2 pumpkin)

Heat oil in a pot. Brown garlic, onion, and tomato. Add pork, season with salt, and cook 5 minutes. Add water or chicken broth and bring to a boil. Add vegetables, cover and cook until vegetables are tender.

Variation: Substitute pork with 18 medium-size shrimp (31- to 40-count), peeled and cleaned. Add shrimp when squash is almost done.

Black Bean Spareribs

yield: 3–4 servings

* *

3 pounds pork spareribs
flour for coating
oil for browning spareribs

Black bean mixture:
2 Tablespoons rinsed and mashed black beans (dau see)
3 cloves garlic, minced
2 Tablespoons soy sauce
2 Tablespoons oyster sauce
1 Tablespoon sugar

Broth mixture:
1 can chicken broth (12-oz.)
1 cup water
1 cube chicken bouillon
1/4 cup cornstarch mixed with 1/4 cup water

Rinse ribs and drain well. Dredge in flour lightly. Heat oil and brown ribs. Add black bean mixture while browning. Add broth mixture (except for cornstarch mixed with 1/4 cup water) and bring to a boil. Stir in cornstarch mixed with water to thicken. Cover and simmer for 45 minutes.

Note: A local favorite that is popular in Chinese restaurants. This recipe is so tasty that it can stand up to any restaurant's recipe.

Sweet-Sour Spareribs

yield: 4 – 6 servings

* *

3 pounds spareribs
1/2 cup flour for coating
3 Tablespoons oil for browning ribs
3/4 cup brown sugar
1 cup water
1 Tablespoon salt
1/2 cup cider vinegar
4 Tablespoons sugar
3 cloves garlic, finely minced

Coat ribs with flour and brown ribs in hot oil. Drain oil. Mix rest of the ingredients and add to ribs. Simmer ribs for 2 hours, or until soft. Stir to prevent sticking.

Variation: Add sliced daikon and carrots to spareribs a few minutes before serving.

Note: Spareribs may be cooked the day before, and refrigerated and the fat removed the next day before serving. My neighbor Audrey got this recipe from her sister-in-law, Ella.

Pork Hash

yield: 2–4 servings

* *

1 pound ground pork
1 teaspoon salt
1 teaspoon cornstarch
1/2 teaspoon sugar
1 teaspoon sherry
1 teaspoon sesame oil
1 Tablespoon soy sauce
1 Tablespoon oyster sauce
1 egg
1 Tablespoon soaked and diced chung choi
4 dried mushrooms, soaked and diced
1/2 cup minced water chestnuts (optional)
2 Tablespoons thinly sliced green onion (optional)

Combine all ingredients and mix well. Place in a large bowl
or platter and flatten. Steam for 45 minutes.

Miso Pork Roast

yield: 4 – 6 servings

* *

4 to 5 pounds pork butt
2 Tablespoons oil

Sauce:
1/2 cup sugar
1/2 cup miso
1/2 cup soy sauce
1/4 cup sake
2 cloves garlic, crushed
1 inch fresh ginger, grated

Combine sauce ingredients; set aside. Heat oil in pot and brown pork all over. Pour sauce over pork. Cover and simmer 3 to 4 hours. Turn over once to prevent sticking. Baste with sauce occasionally.

Note: Ever since Jennie Lee told me about her very popular Miso Pork Roast which she often prepares for her girls from the Puamana Hula Studio, I've been looking for the recipe for miso pork roast. It sounded so delicious. Jenny didn't have the exact measurements, so I tried this recipe which brought very favorable comments. The pork is tasty and juicy with a hint of miso flavor.

Roast Pork

yield: 8 servings

* *

3 pounds pork butt
salt, pepper, and garlic salt to season

Place pork butt on foil-lined 9 × 13 pan. Season with salt, pepper, and garlic salt. Preheat oven to 350°F and bake for 35 minutes per pound. Slice roast pork 1/4-inch thick and serve with your favorite gravy.

Note: An everyday local favorite that is so easy to prepare!

*Mushroom Pork Chops

yield: 3–4 servings

* *

6 pork chops
oil for browning
salt, pepper, and garlic salt to season
1 can cream of mushroom soup (10.75-oz.)
1-1/2 cups milk

Season pork chops with salt, pepper, and garlic salt. Heat oil and brown pork chops. Place in a foil-lined 9 × 13 pan. Combine soup with milk. Pour mixture over pork chops. Place in preheated 350°F oven and bake for 1 hour.

Note: A quick and easy favorite for the busy family during the weekdays.

Pork-Tofu Casserole

yield: 6–8 servings

* *

1 pound lean ground pork
1 teaspoon oil
8 dried mushrooms, soaked and sliced
1 onion, sliced
1 can water chestnuts (8-oz.), drained and chopped
2 Tablespoons sake
1/4 teaspoon salt
1/4 cup soy sauce
2 Tablespoons sugar
1 block firm tofu (20-oz.), cut into 1-inch cubes
2 large eggs, beaten
2 stalks green onion, chopped

Fry pork in oil; add mushrooms, onions, and water chestnuts; sauté until pork is browned. Add sake, salt, soy sauce, and sugar; stir to mix well. Place tofu cubes in bottom of a 3-quart glass casserole dish or 9 × 13 pan coated with vegetable spray. Pour pork mixture over tofu. Pour eggs evenly over pork mixture. Sprinkle green onion over. Cover with foil and bake at 350°F for 35 minutes.

Variation: Substitute pork with ground turkey. Add 1/4 cup bamboo shoots, sliced, with the mushrooms and onions.

Ma Po Tofu (Pork Tofu)

yield: 2–3 servings

* *

1/4 pound ground pork
2 Tablespoons oil
1/8 cup dried shrimps, soaked and drained
1/2 cup chicken broth
1 block firm tofu (20-oz.), cut into 1×2-inch cubes
1 stalk green onion, finely cut for garnish
Chinese parsley, cut in 1-inch lengths for garnish

Sauce:
2 Tablespoons cornstarch
2 Tablespoons water
2 Tablespoons soy sauce
1 Tablespoon oyster sauce
1 teaspoon Hawaiian salt, or less
1 teaspoon chili garlic sauce

Heat oil; sauté pork hash and dried shrimps. Add broth. Bring to a boil; simmer, covered, for 5 minutes. Add tofu and stir lightly until well heated. Add sauce mixture and heat until thickened. Garnish.

Note: Add more chicken broth if gravy is too thick.

Chicken Cacciatore

yield: 4 servings

* *

2 pounds chicken thighs, skinless and boneless
1 cup flour
1 teaspoon salt
1 teaspoon black pepper
1 teaspoon paprika
olive oil for frying
1 onion, thinly sliced in rings or half circles
1 large can tomato sauce (15-oz.)
1 large can whole tomatoes (28-oz.), cut in quarters, Do Not Drain
1 to 2 green peppers, wedged
2 bay leaves
2 teaspoons oregano

Combine flour, salt, pepper, and paprika in a bowl. Coat chicken in flour mixture. In a large, deep skillet, add enough olive oil to brown onions; remove onions. Add more oil as needed and cook floured chicken until golden brown and cooked through. Return onions to the pan. Add rest of the ingredients. Simmer, covered, for 1 to 2 hours.

Suggestion: Serve over hot linguine or hot rice.

Note: This is the best Chicken Cacciatore recipe I've found. It's full flavored and very tomato sauce rich.

Cashew Chicken

yield: 4 – 6 servings

* *

1-1/2 pounds boneless chicken, cut into 1-inch cubes
1 cup cashews
3 stalks celery, cut into 1-inch cubes
2 carrots, cut into 1/2-inch cubes, microwaved 2 minutes
1 green pepper, cut into 1-inch cubes
1 onion, cut into 1-inch cubes
oil for frying

Seasoning:
1/2 teaspoon salt
1/2 teaspoon sugar
1/2 teaspoon pepper
1 Tablespoon sesame oil
1 Tablespoon oil
1 egg white

Combine seasoning ingredients; marinate chicken with seasoning and refrigerate for 2 hours. Heat oil in a skillet and brown chicken. Remove chicken. Stir-fry vegetables until crisp tender; add chicken and cashews. Toss together.

Note: My sister-in-law's (Amy) family recipe. One of the best Cashew Chicken recipes that I have tasted, it is also a healthy dish for the family.

Chicken Chili

yield: 10–12 servings

* *

2 pounds ground chicken
2 Tablespoons oil
1 to 2 onions, diced
4 cloves garlic, minced
2 cans red kidney beans (14.5-oz. each)
1 can diced stewed tomatoes (14.5-oz.)
2 cans tomato sauce (8-oz. each)
4 to 5 Tablespoons chili powder
2 teaspoons garlic salt
2 teaspoons oregano
2 teaspoons cumin
2 teaspoons black pepper

Heat oil and brown chicken in a large pot. Add onions and garlic and cook, covered, until onions are soft. Add all other ingredients and simmer, covered, on low heat for 2 hours, stirring occasionally.

Note: For spicier chili, add 1 teaspoon crushed red pepper and 1/2 teaspoon cayenne pepper.

Chicken Enchilada

yield: 8–10 enchiladas

* *

3 to 4 pounds chicken thighs, skinless and boneless
1 medium onion, diced
salt to season
2 packages cream cheese (8-oz. each)
1/2 pint whipping cream
1 package flour tortilla, 10 count (16-oz.)
1 can Las Palmas® Green Chili Enchilada Sauce (19-oz.)
2 to 3 cups shredded cheddar cheese
salsa for topping (select your favorite salsa)

Boil chicken and shred; place in a large bowl. Add onion and sprinkle salt to taste. In a separate bowl, combine cream cheese and whipping cream. Mix until smooth. Add to chicken and onion; mix together. Place filling onto each tortilla and roll up. Place on greased 9 × 13 pan. (8 to 10 rolls should fit, depending on thickness of rolls.) Pour enchilada sauce over and sprinkle cheese on top. Bake at 350°F for 30 minutes. Serve with salsa.

Note: My niece Donna Watanabe introduced me to this great-tasting enchilada. I shared it with my neighbor, who then shared it at a potluck. It's very rich, so I usually cut each piece in half.

Chicken Adobo

yield: 6–8 servings

* *

3 pounds chicken thighs, skinless, cut in half with bone
1/2 cup white vinegar
1/2 cup soy sauce
1 teaspoon brown sugar
2 Tablespoons peppercorns, crush about half
5 cloves garlic, crushed
3 bay leaves
salt to season

Combine all ingredients in a pan; cover and marinate 1 to 3 hours. Bring to a boil, then lower heat and simmer for 30 minutes. Remove cover and simmer for an additional 15 minutes, or until most of the liquid has evaporated and the chicken is lightly brown.

Note: This is the best Chicken Adobo I've ever tasted.

*Chicken Katsu

yield: 6 servings

* *

2 pounds chicken breasts, boneless and skinless
garlic salt to season
1/2 cup flour
2 eggs, beaten
2 cups panko flakes (flour meal for breading)
oil for frying

Katsu sauce:
1/3 cup catsup
1/4 cup soy sauce, or less
1/4 cup sugar
1-1/2 teaspoons Worcestershire® sauce
pinch of ground red pepper

Combine all katsu sauce ingredients; mix well. Set aside.

Season chicken generously with garlic salt and let stand 15 to 30 minutes. Heat about 1/2 inch of oil in a skillet. Dredge chicken in flour, dip in eggs, and coat with panko in that order. Fry chicken until golden brown on both sides; drain on paper towels. Cut into 1-inch slices. Serve with katsu sauce.

Note: This is so-o-o good! The chicken is tender inside and light and crispy on the outside. Kristen Hasegawa's favorite!

Flavored Chicken
for Chinese Stir-fry

yield: 4–6 servings

* *

**1-1/2 pounds boneless, skinless chicken thighs or breasts,
cut into slices (about 6 thighs)**
**1 pound vegetables (green beans, asparagus, choi sum,
won bok, Chinese peas, etc. or any desired vegetable
combinations)**

Marinade:
2 Tablespoons soy sauce
1 Tablespoon sugar
2 Tablespoons cornstarch
2 Tablespoons oyster sauce
1 to 2 Tablespoons sesame oil
1 Tablespoon sherry

Marinate chicken for 30 minutes or longer. (May be refrigerated overnight.) Fry with any vegetable available.

Heat enough oil in a pan or wok (about 1 tablespoon) to stir-fry vegetables. Quickly stir-fry vegetables; sprinkle with salt to season. Do not overcook. Remove from pan. Add 1 tablespoon oil to the same pan and heat. Fry chicken until just done; add vegetables and quickly toss together.

Note: Marinade can also be used for sliced beef and stir-fried with vegetables. This is your all-time basic marinade for any stir-fry dish.

Chicken Long Rice

yield: 6 – 8 servings

* *

2 pounds chicken thighs, skinless and boneless
2 Tablespoons oil
1 clove garlic, crushed
1-inch piece fresh ginger, crushed
1 onion, sliced
2 cans chicken broth (14.5-oz. each)
2 bundles long rice (2-oz. each), soaked in hot water
pepper to season
1 stalk green onion, cut in 2-inch lengths

Cut chicken into bite-sized pieces (about 1-1/2-inch pieces). Sauté garlic and ginger in oil. Add onion and chicken, and fry until slightly browned. Add chicken broth; bring to a boil. Skim off fat and residue. Lower heat and simmer for 40 minutes.

Cut soaked long rice into 3- to 4-inch lengths. Add long rice, pepper, and green onion to chicken simmering in broth and cook 10 minutes longer.

Variation: Cut a tomato in wedges and simmer together with long rice for added flavor.

Note: Rachel Hasegawa's favorite! This is the easiest to prepare.

Gay's Easy Potluck Chicken

yield: 16–18 servings

* *

**5 pounds frozen chicken thighs, skinless and
    boneless (NOT thawed)**
3 cups catsup
3 cups soy sauce
3 cups sugar
5 cloves garlic, grated
3-inch piece fresh ginger, grated

Place frozen chicken pieces in large roasting pan (i.e., Hefty Roaster Pan for up to 20 pounds: 16-1/8 × 11-3/4 × 2-7/8), to allow for liquid from chicken. Combine rest of ingredients; pour over chicken. Bake at 350°F for 2 hours. Turn chicken over once or twice to marinade all over. If desired, cut into smaller pieces when done.

Note: Gay Iijima thinks this is the easiest way to prepare for a potluck. She's made this often, and everyone loves the taste.

Yakitori

yield: 4 servings

* *

**2 pounds chicken thighs, boneless and skinless,
    cut into 1-1/2-inch squares**
1/4 cup sugar, or less
5 Tablespoons soy sauce
1 Tablespoon sherry or sake
1/2 teaspoon salt
1 teaspoon sesame oil
1 clove garlic, crushed

Blend all ingredients (except chicken). Soak chicken in sauce overnight. Charcoal, pan fry, or skewer, if desired, with onion and green pepper and broil.

Fried Chicken

yield: 4–6 servings

* *

3 pounds chicken parts
1 Tablespoon Hawaiian salt (or less)
1 egg, beaten
1/2 teaspoon salt
oil for frying, 1-inch deep

Flour mixture:
2 cups cornstarch
1/2 cup flour
1 Tablespoon garlic salt
1 teaspoon pepper

Rub Hawaiian salt all over chicken and let set for 30 minutes.

Heat oil in a large, heavy skillet on medium-high heat (350°F).

Combine flour mixture in plastic bag. Mix egg and 1/2 teaspoon salt together. Dip chicken in egg. Place in flour mixture and shake well until coated. Place skin side down in the skillet. Turn chicken over when brown and cook until done. Test for doneness before removing from oil. Drain on paper towel.

Note: One of my sister-in-law's (Evie) favorite family recipes passed down from her mother. The outside of the chicken is crispy and the inside juicy and moist.

Cold Chicken
with Ginger Sauce

yield: 4–6 servings

* *

2 quarts water
1 Tablespoon salt
1-inch piece ginger
4 pounds frying or roasting chicken
Chinese parsley, chopped (optional)

Ginger Sauce:
1 Tablespoon Hawaiian salt
1 clove garlic, finely minced
1/3 cup finely minced ginger
1/3 cup minced green onion
1/2 cup salad oil

Boil water, salt, and 1-inch piece ginger. Add whole chicken, cover, and immediately turn to lowest heat for 30 minutes. Turn chicken over; cover the pot for another 30 minutes at lowest heat. Remove chicken and rinse quickly with cold water or let sit in cold water until chicken is cool. Drain and refrigerate. Cut chicken in 2 × 1-inch pieces and place in a serving dish. Refrigerate.

In a small bowl, combine salt, garlic, ginger, and green onion. Heat oil and pour over green onion mixture; mix well. Pour sauce over chicken pieces. Garnish with parsley, if desired.

Note: Chicken must be fresh and not frozen for best results.

Lemon Chicken

yield: 4–6 servings

* *

1-1/2 pounds boneless chicken breasts, cut into
 2 × 1-1/2-inch pieces
1 Tablespoon sherry
1-1/2 teaspoons soy sauce
1 cup cornstarch
1/2 cup milk
2 cups salad oil

Marinate chicken in sherry and soy sauce for 10 minutes. Dredge in cornstarch, dip in milk; dredge in cornstarch again. Fry in oil heated to 350°F for about 3 minutes or until golden brown. Drain on paper towel.

Lemon Sauce:
3/4 cup water
1/4 cup white distilled vinegar
1/2 cup sugar
1 Tablespoon lemon juice
1/2 teaspoon salt
1/8 teaspoon yellow food color
2 Tablespoons cornstarch, blended with equal amount of water
5 thin lemon slices

Mix all sauce ingredients (except cornstarch and lemon slices). Cook over medium-high heat, stirring constantly, until mixture comes to a boil. Stir in cornstarch mixture. Add lemon slices and cook an extra minute. Pour over chicken; arrange lemon slices attractively.

Shoyu Chicken

yield: 3–4 servings

* *

6 chicken thighs, with bone and skin
1/2 cup sugar
1/2 cup soy sauce
1 clove garlic, grated (optional)
1-inch piece ginger, grated (optional)

Place all ingredients in pot; bring to boil. Lower heat, cover and simmer for about 30 to 40 minutes.

Suggestion: Serve with rice, corn, and a vegetable salad for a satisfying local dinner.

Note: My daughter, Cheryl, gave this recipe to me. It has its roots in Popo Hee. To make the sauce, she would get a large saimin bowl, pour soy sauce in it, spoon some sugar, and add ginger, garlic, and sometimes a little water if the sauce seemed too strong. Her children loved her shoyu chicken.

Easy Roast Chicken

yield: 2–4 servings

* *

2 to 3 pounds fryer
Hawaiian salt to season
1 clove garlic, grated (optional)

Rinse fryer and pat dry. Rub Hawaiian salt (and garlic, if desired) in cavity and all over chicken. Place in a pan or CorningWare®. Bake at 400°F for 1 hour.

Note: At 'Aikahi Elementary, this is known as Lorna's Chicken because Lorna Tam Ho shared her roast chicken recipe.

Mochiko Chicken

yield: 4 servings

* *

2 pounds chicken thighs, deboned
4 Tablespoons mochiko
4 Tablespoons cornstarch
4 Tablespoons sugar
5 Tablespoons soy sauce
2 cloves garlic, minced
1/2 teaspoon salt
2 eggs, beaten
1/4 cup thinly sliced green onion
1 Tablespoon sesame seeds (optional)
1/2 teaspoon grated ginger
oil for frying

Mix everything (except chicken and oil). Marinate chicken for 5 hours or overnight in the refrigerator. Fry chicken in 1-inch hot oil until golden brown on both sides. Serve hot or cold. When cold, may be cut into slices.

Note: Definitely a local favorite for parties, picnics, and tailgating.

McCarthy's Marinade

yield: 3–5 servings

* *

2 pounds lamb rib chops

Marinade:
1/4 cup olive oil
3 Tablespoons balsamic vinegar
6 to 7 cloves garlic, finely minced
1 Tablespoon thyme
1 teaspoon salt
1/4 teaspoon pepper

Combine ingredients and mix together. Place lamb rib chops in a plastic bag with marinade and seal. Marinate overnight. Grill over hibachi to preferred doneness.

Note: Liz McCarthy, mother of Stephanie M. (I also had Stephanie G. in my kindergarten class at 'Aikahi many years ago), gave me this favorite family marinade recipe while standing in line at a supermarket one day.

Butter Yaki

yield: 4 servings

* *

1 pound tender meat, thinly sliced
1 pound chicken breasts, boneless and skinless,
   thinly sliced
1 package bean sprouts (10-oz.)
1 onion, thinly sliced
1 zucchini, cut into 2-1/2-inch lengths, then cut into "sticks"
1 tray mushrooms (8-oz.), sliced
1/2 block butter

Sauce:
1/4 cup soy sauce
1/4 cup mirin
1/4 cup sugar
1/4 cup daikon, peeled and grated
1/4 cup apple, peeled and grated
2 limes, cut in halves (optional)

Prepare sauce first. Cook all sauce ingredients, except for limes, for a few minutes. Cool and set aside in 4 individual serving dishes. (Individuals may squeeze in own lime juice, if preferred, before dipping cooked meat and vegetables into the sauce.)

Use an electric skillet set at 250°F at dinner table. (Temperature may be adjusted while you cook.) Add some butter to skillet and place some bean sprouts and onion slices to begin cooking. When bean sprouts and onions are about half done, add mushrooms and zucchini slices, adding more butter as needed. Cook thinly sliced meat and chicken last. Eat while it is hot, dipping in individual dishes of prepared sauce. Add more vegetables and meat in skillet.

Variation: Add other types of vegetables, such as Chinese cabbage, green onion, and watercress, cut in 2-inch lengths.

Note: This is a family favorite! The sauce is yummy and everything is freshly cooked and hot.

Baked Fish

yield: 4 servings

* *

2 pounds fish fillets
juice of 1 lemon
garlic salt and pepper to season
1 cup mayonnaise
1/4 cup finely chopped onion
bread crumbs for topping

Squeeze lemon juice on fish. Sprinkle with garlic salt and pepper. Place fish in a foil-lined baking pan. Mix mayonnaise and chopped onion together; spread on fish. Sprinkle with bread crumbs. Bake at 425°F for 20 to 25 minutes.

Note: Fish can be marinated overnight (without bread crumbs).

Miso Butterfish

yield: 4 servings

* *

4 butterfish fillets
3/4 cup miso
1/3 cup sake or sherry

Dry butterfish with paper towel. Mix miso and sake into a paste. Marinate fish in paste overnight. Broil until brown.

Note: Tastes wonderful and is so easy to prepare!

Honey-Glazed Walnut Shrimp

yield: 4 servings

* *

1/2 pound large shrimp or prawns, cleaned and deveined
2 cups water
1 cup walnut halves
4 cups water
1/2 cup sugar
1/4 cup honey
oil for frying
2 egg whites, beaten
flour for coating
1/2 Tablespoon vinegar
2 Tablespoons mayonnaise
1 Tablespoon sweetened condensed milk
1 Tablespoon sugar
1 Tablespoon roasted sesame seeds for garnish (optional)

Bring 2 cups water to boiling. Add walnuts; cook for 10 minutes. Drain.

Bring 4 cups water and 1/2 cup sugar to a boil. Add blanched walnuts and cook for 10 more minutes. Drain. Combine walnuts and honey. Heat oil in a wok and fry walnuts for 1 to 2 minutes or until brown.

Dip shrimp in egg whites; coat with flour. Heat oil in the wok and fry shrimp for 1 to 2 minutes. Remove shrimp and drain oil from wok. In the same hot wok, combine remaining ingredients; add shrimp and cook for 1 minute. Serve with walnuts.

Note: A local favorite that is gaining popularity in the fast-food plate lunch venues.

'Ōpakapaka
with Chinese Cabbage

yield: 2–4 servings

* *

'Ōpakapaka, whole fish, cleaned (cut in half if too large)
salt and pepper to season
flour for dredging
2 Tablespoons oil for frying fish
1 stalk green onion, finely chopped

Gravy with vegetables:
2 Tablespoons chung choi, rinsed and chopped
4 pieces shiitake mushrooms, soaked and sliced (save
    mushroom water)
1 small head Chinese cabbage, cut in 1-1/4-inch slices
1 piece each garlic and ginger, crushed
1 teaspoon salt
1 teaspoon soy sauce
1 teaspoon sugar
1-1/4 cups mushroom water
2 Tablespoons cornstarch mixed with equal amount water

Sprinkle salt and pepper on fish. Coat with flour and fry in
hot oil. When fish is cooked, place on a serving platter and
immediately sprinkle green onion over fish. Set aside.

In the same frying pan used to cook fish, fry chung choi and
mushrooms. Add Chinese cabbage. When almost done, add
garlic, ginger, seasonings, and mushroom water. Thicken
with cornstarch and water mixture. Pour Chinese cabbage
and gravy over fried fish.

*Note: This is a very old recipe that my mom gave me and
everyone loves it! The original recipe used mullet, but I prefer
'ōpakapaka. If I see fresh 'ōpakapaka at the supermarket the
right size for my frying pan (sometimes I'll cut off the tail
to have it fit), I'll change my menu for that night's meal and
head to the produce department for Chinese cabbage.*

Chinese Steamed Fish

yield: 3–4 servings

* *

3 pounds whole fish, cleaned with head and tail on
Soy sauce to season
1/2 cup finely chopped green onion
1/4 cup finely chopped fresh ginger
1/4 cup finely chopped chung choi
1 cup peanut oil, heated

Pour small amount of soy sauce in the cavity of the cleaned fish. Steam fish for 20 to 25 minutes in a steam pan. When fish is steamed, remove and place on a platter. Mix together green onion, ginger, and chung choi and place over fish. Pour hot sizzling peanut oil over chopped ingredients and fish. Serve immediately.

Variation: If an elongated fish steamer pan is unavailable, chop fish into large pieces to fit in a bowl and place in a round-type steamer.

Note: ʻŌpakapaka (red snapper), kūmū, or other fish that steams well tastes best. A healthy and tasty alternative in preparing fish.

Shrimp Curry

yield: 3–5 servings

* *

1-1/2 pounds shrimp, cleaned
1 onion, chopped
3 cloves garlic, minced
4 Tablespoons butter
2 cups water (or 1 can coconut milk and water to
    equal 2 cups)
2 large tomatoes, peeled and chopped
2 stalks celery, sliced
1 Tablespoon shredded coconut
1 piece ginger, crushed
1/4 teaspoon ground ginger
1 Tablespoon sugar
1-1/2 Tablespoons curry powder
1-1/2 Tablespoons flour
1-1/2 teaspoons salt
1/4 teaspoon pepper

Sauté onion and garlic in butter until lightly browned. Add water or coconut milk and bring to a boil. Add tomatoes, celery, coconut, and fresh ginger. Blend ground ginger with sugar, curry powder, flour, salt, and pepper. Add enough cold water to moisten into a paste and add to boiling mixture. Simmer, stirring occasionally, until vegetables are tender. Add shrimp; cook for 5 minutes.

Suggestion: Serve with condiments such as chutney, peanuts, boiled eggs, green onions, and bacon bits.

Variation: Substitute shrimp with scallops or crab legs.

Hint: To peel tomatoes, place tomatoes in boiling water for 1 to 2 minutes. Remove and cool in cold water. Skin can then be easily peeled off.

*Butterfish with Shoyu Sauce

yield: 3–4 servings

* *

1 pound butterfish
salt and pepper to season
flour for dredging
1 to 2 Tablespoons oil

Sauce:
1/4 cup soy sauce
5 Tablespoons sugar
1 stalk green onion, chopped
1 large clove garlic, minced
chili pepper or crushed red pepper to season (optional)

Combine sauce ingredients and mix well.

Salt and pepper butterfish. Dredge in flour and fry. When done, soak in sauce while still hot. Serve or simmer in sauce for a few minutes before serving.

Note: My mom gave me this recipe, and it's become a family favorite!

Easy Seafood Pasta

yield: 5–6 servings

* *

1 box bowtie pasta (12-oz.), cook according to directions
1 pound frozen cooked shrimp (51- to 60-count)
2 Tablespoons olive oil
2 cloves garlic, minced
1/2 cup white wine
Salt and pepper to taste
2 Tablespoons butter
Mozzarella, for sprinkling
Parmesan cheese, for sprinkling
Parsley, chopped, for sprinkling

Sauce:
1-1/2 cups prepared pasta sauce, any brand (i.e., Prego, Fresh Mushroom Sauce)
1/2 cup red wine
2 Tablespoons brown sugar
2 Tablespoons olive oil

Prepare sauce; set aside.

In deep pot, heat 2 tablespoons olive oil. Add garlic and lightly brown. Add shrimp and white wine. Add salt and pepper; simmer for few minutes. Add sauce and mix together. Add pasta and mix well; heat through. Add 2 tablespoons butter to mixture before serving. Sprinkle mozzarella, Parmesan cheese, and parsley, if desired.

Note: While book-signing in Hilo, I met Eva Kawasaki Takaki, my classmate from Hilo High, class of '57. I hadn't seen her since we graduated! It was great chatting with her and when I asked about her favorite recipe, she shared this easy pasta dish. It's delicious!

*Furikake Salmon

yield: 2 servings

* *

1 fillet of salmon
mayonnaise for spreading
furikake for sprinkling
1 Tablespoon butter

Cut fillet into portion sizes. Generously spread mayonnaise on one side of salmon. Sprinkle furikake generously over mayonnaise. Heat pan on medium heat and add butter. Place salmon furikake-side down, lower heat to medium-low, and slowly cook for 10 to 15 minutes. While cooking, spread mayonnaise and furikake on top. Turn over and cook other side.

Optional: If desired, serve cooked salmon with the following sauce.

Sauce:
2 Tablespoons butter
2 cloves garlic, minced
1/4 cup soy sauce
2 Tablespoons sugar

Melt butter, add garlic, and stir. Blend in soy sauce and sugar, and simmer for 1 to 2 minutes. Pour over cooked salmon.

Note: This is a local-style salmon that is so tasty. Thanks to Donna Watanabe who gave me this recipe.

Shrimp with
Black Bean Sauce

yield: 4 servings

* *

1 pound shrimp, peeled
1 Tablespoon oil
1 onion, cut into 1-inch pieces
1 green pepper, seeded and cubed
salt to season
2 cloves garlic, crushed
green onion, chopped, or Chinese parsley for garnish (optional)

Sauce:
1 clove garlic, minced
1 teaspoon grated fresh ginger
2 Tablespoons rinsed and mashed salted black beans
1 Tablespoon sherry
1 Tablespoon soy sauce
1/2 cup chicken broth
1 teaspoon sugar
2 teaspoons cornstarch with 1 Tablespoon water
dash of sesame oil

In a frying pan or wok, heat oil and stir-fry onion and bell pepper with a sprinkle of salt, until vegetables are crisp-tender. Remove. In the same pan, add a little oil as needed and sauté garlic. Add shrimp; cook until pink. Remove shrimp and discard garlic.

In the same pan, add a little oil as needed, and sauté minced garlic, ginger, and black bean. Add sherry, soy sauce, chicken broth, and sugar. Bring to a boil; stir in cornstarch mixture and sesame oil. When sauce thickens, add reserved onion, pepper, and shrimp. Heat through and serve. Garnish with green onion or Chinese parsley.

Spanish Rice

yield: 6–8 servings

* *

1 pound lean ground beef
1 to 2 cloves garlic, minced
1 small onion, chopped
1 Tablespoon oil
1 green pepper, chopped
2 Tablespoons chili powder
1/2 teaspoon salt
1/4 teaspoon pepper
1/2 teaspoon oregano
1 can stewed tomatoes (14.5-oz.)
1 can pitted olives (6-oz.), undrained, keep whole or
   cut in slices
1-1/2 cups uncooked rice, rinsed and drained

In a large skillet, heat oil and sauté garlic and onions. Add ground beef, green pepper, chili powder, salt, pepper, and oregano. Cook until ground beef is done. Add rice and cook for 3 minutes. Add stewed tomatoes, breaking up tomatoes into smaller pieces. Mix in olives with liquid. Add just enough water to cover. Simmer with lid on until rice is cooked, taking care not to burn rice (about 40 minutes or until done). Stir occasionally while cooking.

Note: Thanks to Gaylynn Kalama for sharing this 'ono Spanish Rice with all of us at 'Aikahi Elementary.

Tofu Burgers

yield: 4–6 servings

* *

1 block firm tofu (20-oz.)
1/2 cup finely grated carrot
1/4 cup finely chopped onion
1 slice bread, crumbled
1 egg
1 Tablespoon chopped green onion (chives or parsley)
oil for frying

Use cheesecloth or clean cotton towel to squeeze tofu dry. Mix with other ingredients. Make patties. Heat a little oil in a pan and cook like burgers.

Note: Top with a slice of cheese or brush on teriyaki sauce.

Oriental-Style Fish

yield: 3–4 servings

* *

2 pounds fish fillet (mahimahi, 'ahi, ono, etc.)
oil for frying

Marinade:
4 Tablespoons flour
8 Tablespoons cornstarch
4 Tablespoons sugar
1-1/2 teaspoons salt
5 Tablespoons soy sauce
2 eggs
2 stalks green onions, chopped
2 cloves garlic, crushed
1 teaspoon sesame seeds
2 teaspoons sesame oil

Combine marinade ingredients and marinate fish for about 1 hour. Heat oil and fry fish.

Stuffed Tofu

yield: 3–4 servings

* *

1 block firm tofu (20-oz.)
3 shrimp (21 to 25 count), cleaned and finely chopped
1/4 pound ground pork
1 slice cooked ham (i.e., from 6-oz. package Oscar Mayer®
    brand), minced
3 water chestnuts, finely chopped
1/2 Tablespoon chung choi, rinsed and finely chopped
1/2 teaspoon salt
1 Tablespoon green onion, chopped (for garnish)

Gravy:
3/4 cup water
2 Tablespoons soy sauce
1/2 teaspoon salt
2 teaspoons sugar
1 Tablespoon cornstarch

Cut tofu into 12 pieces and slit each piece halfway; set aside. Combine rest of ingredients (except green onion); mix well and divide into 12 portions. Slightly flatten each portion and fill each tofu slit. Place in steaming dish. Combine gravy ingredients in small saucepan and heat to thicken slightly. Pour over stuffed tofu. Steam for 30 minutes. Garnish with chopped green onions.

Note: This is another favorite local recipe enjoyed by many! It was given to me by Fumiko Ando when we first began our teaching career in Kamuela on the Big Island.

Desserts

Chocolate Banana Bread

yield: two 9 × 5 loaf pans

* *

4 eggs
1-1/2 cups sugar
1 cup salad oil
2-1/2 cups flour
2 teaspoons baking powder
2 teaspoons baking soda
1 teaspoon salt
3 cups mashed bananas (about 5 to 6 bananas)
1 teaspoon lemon juice
1/2 cup chocolate chips
1/2 cup nuts, chopped

Beat eggs and add oil. Sift dry ingredients together and add to egg mixture. Blend well. Add lemon juice to banana and add to the mixture; mix well. Add nuts and chocolate chips. Pour into 2 greased loaf pans. Bake* at 350°F for 55 minutes, or until done. (Test with wooden skewer.)

*You may use 6 baby loaf pans (5.75 × 3.25 × 2), bake at 350°F for 35 to 40 minutes.

Note: Chocolate chips add a special taste to the banana bread. Pūʻōhala teachers taste-tested this and gave it a "thumbs up." It also tastes great without the chocolate chips!

Watergate Cake

yield: 24 servings

* *

1 box yellow cake mix
1 box instant pistachio pudding mix (3.5-oz)
3 eggs, room temperature
1 cup salad oil
1 cup 7 Up®, room temperature
1/2 cup chocolate chips
1/2 cup walnuts, chopped

In a large bowl, mix together cake mix, pudding, eggs, and oil. Add 7 Up® and mix for 1 minute. Add chocolate chips. Grease and flour bundt pan. Put walnuts into pan, then pour batter over nuts. Bake at 350°F for 40 to 50 minutes.

Icing (optional):
2 envelopes nondairy whipped topping mix
    (1.5-oz each)
1 package instant pistachio pudding mix
1-1/2 cups milk

Beat all ingredients in bowl until smooth and thick. Spread over cooled cake.

Note: If using greased and floured 9 × 13 pan, bake at 350°F for 35 to 45 minutes or until done. A time-tested recipe that is still a family and office favorite after 25 years.

Bacardi® Rum Cake

yield: 24 servings

* *

1 box yellow cake mix
1 package instant vanilla pudding (3-oz.)
4 eggs
1/2 cup cold water
1/2 cup oil
1/4 cup Bacardi® dark rum (80 proof)
1 cup pecans or walnuts, chopped

In large bowl, mix all ingredients together, except nuts. Sprinkle nuts over bottom of greased and floured 10-inch tube pan or 12-cup bundt pan. Pour batter over nuts. Bake at 325°F for 1 hour. Cool. Invert on serving plate then glaze.

Glaze:
1/2 cup butter
1/4 cup water
1 cup sugar
1/4 cup Bacardi® dark rum

Melt butter in saucepan. Stir in water and sugar. Boil 5 minutes, stirring constantly. Remove from heat. Stir in rum. Prick top of cake. Drizzle and smooth the glaze evenly over top and sides. Allow cake to absorb glaze.

Optional: Decorate with whole maraschino cherries and a border of whipped cream.

Note: If you are unsure of what dessert to bring to a potluck, this is always a sure bet to be a winner and is easy to make.

Cocoa Cake

yield: 24–30 servings

* *

2-1/2 cups flour
1-1/2 cups sugar
1/2 cup cocoa
2 teaspoons baking soda, sifted
1/2 teaspoon salt
2/3 cup oil
2 Tablespoons white vinegar
1 Tablespoon vanilla
2 cups cold coffee or cold water

Topping:
1/4 cup sugar
1/2 teaspoon cinnamon

Mix first 5 ingredients. Stir with fork to mix. Add next 4 ingredients and stir with fork until well mixed. DO NOT BEAT. Pour into ungreased 9×13 pan. Combine sugar and cinnamon; sprinkle over batter. Bake at 350°F for 30 to 35 minutes.

Note: This chocolate cake is so moist that it doesn't need frosting. Linda Kealoha, a teacher, has shared this recipe many times at school potlucks because it is such a favorite with the faculty.

Chiffon Cake

yield: 10–12 servings

* *

2 cups flour, sifted
1-1/2 cups sugar
3 teaspoons baking powder
1 teaspoon salt
1/2 cup oil
6 large egg yolks, unbeaten
3/4 cup cold water
2 teaspoons almond extract
1/2 teaspoon cream of tartar
1 cup egg whites (from 8 large eggs)

Sift first four ingredients together. Make a well and add oil, egg yolks, water, and almond extract. Beat until smooth. (With electric mixer, use medium speed for 1 minute.) In large bowl, add cream of tartar to egg whites; beat at high speed for 3 to 5 minutes until whites form very stiff peaks. Do not underbeat. Preheat oven to 325°F.

Pour egg yolk mixture gradually over beaten egg whites, gently folding with rubber spatula just until blended. Do not stir. Pour immediately into ungreased 10-inch tube pan. Bake at 325°F for 55 minutes, then increase to 350°F for 10 to 15 minutes, or until top springs back when lightly touched. Turn pan upside down, placing tube over neck of funnel or bottle. Let hang until cold. Loosen with spatula. Turn pan over, hit edge sharply on table to loosen.

Note: A very light cake. This recipe was passed down from Aunty Clara (Chun) and is so often requested that someone always makes it for family gatherings.

Kahlúa® Cake

yield: 24-30 servings

✳ ✳

1 box yellow cake mix
1 package instant chocolate pudding
4 eggs
1 cup oil
1/4 cup Kahlúa® liqueur
3/4 cup water

Mix all ingredients for 3 minutes. Pour into 9 × 13 pan.
Bake at 350°F for 50 minutes or until done.

Topping:
1/2 cup powdered sugar
1/4 cup Kahlúa® liqueur
1 teaspoon instant coffee, powdery texture

Mix and let sit. Prick cake before pouring topping over cake.

Note: This cake tastes great even without topping.

Mango Bread

yield: 9 × 5 loaf pan

* *

2 cups flour
2 teaspoons baking soda
1 teaspoon baking powder
2 teaspoons cinnamon
1/2 teaspoon salt
1 cup sugar
1/4 cup oil
1/2 cup butter or margarine, melted
1/4 cup nuts, chopped
1 teaspoon vanilla
1-3/4 cup mangoes, finely chopped
3 eggs, beaten
1/2 cup raisins

Sift dry ingredients together into a large bowl. Make a well and place all other ingredients into well; mix. Pour into a greased 9 × 5 loaf pan and let stand for 20 minutes. Bake* at 350°F for 45 minutes to 1 hour, or until done.

*You may use 4 greased baby loaf pans (5.75 × 3.25 × 2), bake at 350°F for 40 to 45 minutes. Test with skewer for doneness.

Carrot Cake

yield: 24–30 servings

* *

4 eggs, beaten
1-1/2 cups sugar
1-1/4 cups salad oil
2 cups flour
2 teaspoons baking powder
1-1/2 teaspoons baking soda
1 teaspoon salt
2 teaspoons cinnamon
4 cups grated carrots
1/2 teaspoon vanilla
3/4 cup nuts, chopped

Beat eggs; add sugar and oil. Separately sift together dry ingredients; add to egg mixture. Beat for 2 minutes. Add carrots, vanilla, and nuts; mix well. Pour into ungreased 9 × 13 pan. Bake at 325°F for 45 to 50 minutes.

Frosting:
1 package cream cheese (8-oz.), softened
1/2 cup butter or margarine, softened
1 teaspoon vanilla
2 cups powdered sugar, sifted

Beat cream cheese and butter until blended; add vanilla and powdered sugar. Beat well until smooth and of spreading consistency. Spread over cooled cake. Refrigerate.

Note: If needed, add milk, a little at a time, to make a spread-able consistency. This recipe is so good that even non-carrot cake lovers like it. It also makes a nice birthday cake because it is so easy to decorate on top of the plain cream cheese frosting.

Corn Bread

yield: 9 × 13 loaf pan

* *

3 cups Bisquick®
1 cup sugar
1/2 cup cornmeal
1/2 teaspoon salt
1 teaspoon baking powder
1-1/2 cups milk
3 eggs
3/4 cup oil
1 Tablespoon vanilla
1/2 cup butter (1 block)

Mix dry ingredients. Add the remaining ingredients, except the butter. Pour into 9 × 13 pan and bake at 350°F for 35 minutes or longer until done. Melt butter and spread over top immediately after baking.

Note: This is the most buttery and moist corn bread recipe that I ever tasted. A definite family favorite!

Creamsicle Cake

yield: 24–30 servings

* *

1 box white cake mix with pudding (i.e. Pillsbury® Moist
Supreme which uses 1 cup water, 1/3 cup oil and 3 eggs)
1 box orange Jell-O® (3-oz.)
1 cup boiling water
1/2 cup cold water

Bake cake according to directions on box. Cool. Dissolve
Jell-O® in boiling water and add cold water. Cool. Use large
end of chopstick to poke holes in cake. Use spoon to pour
Jell-O® over cake and into holes.

Frosting:
1 box instant vanilla pudding (3-oz.)
1 cup milk
1 container Cool Whip® (8-oz.)
1 teaspoon vanilla
1 teaspoon orange extract

Beat vanilla pudding and milk until thickened. Mix in Cool
Whip®, vanilla, and orange extract until well blended. Frost
cake and refrigerate.

Note: Fantastic! Tastes like an ice cream cake and is super
easy to prepare.

Poppy Seed Bundt Cake

yield: 10-inch bundt cake pan

* *

1 box yellow cake mix
1 box instant vanilla pudding (3-oz.)
1/2 teaspoon baking powder
2 Tablespoons poppy seeds
3/4 cup vegetable oil
1 teaspoon almond extract
1 cup hot water
4 eggs

Mix dry ingredients; add oil. Blend in eggs, one at a time. Add hot water and extract. Bake in greased and floured bundt pan or 9 × 13 pan at 300°F for about 50 minutes.

Sour Cream Chocolate Cake

yield: 24 – 30 servings

* *

1 box chocolate cake mix (or devil's food chocolate cake mix)
1 box instant vanilla pudding or chocolate pudding mix (3-oz.)
4 eggs
3/4 cup salad oil
1/3 cup Kahlúa® (optional)
1 pint sour cream (2 cups)
1/2 cup chocolate chips (optional)

Combine cake mix and instant pudding. In a separate bowl, beat eggs and add oil, Kahlúa®, and sour cream. Beat well. Add to cake mixture and mix thoroughly. Mix in chocolate chips. Pour into greased and floured bundt pan (or lightly greased 9 × 13 pan). Bake at 350°F for 45 to 60 minutes.

Mandarin Peach Cake

yield: 24–30 servings

* *

1 box yellow cake mix
1 cup oil
4 eggs
1 can mandarin oranges (11-oz.), Do Not Drain

Mix all ingredients except mandarin oranges and beat at medium speed until well blended. Add mandarin oranges with juice and beat until oranges are slightly mashed. Pour into greased 9 × 13 pan and bake at 350°F for 35 to 40 minutes, or until done. Cool.

Frosting:
1 box instant vanilla pudding mix (3-oz.)
1 can sliced peaches (15-oz.), drained
1 container Cool Whip® (8-oz.)

Chop sliced peaches and place in bowl. Use electric mixer to mash peaches. Add vanilla pudding and beat together. Fold in Cool Whip® and blend. Frost cake.

Pumpkin Crunch

yield: 9 × 13 pan

* *

1 can solid-packed pumpkin (29-oz.)
1 can evaporated milk (13-oz.)
1 cup sugar
3 eggs, slightly beaten
1/4 teaspoon cinnamon
1 box yellow pudding cake mix
1 cup walnuts, chopped
1 cup butter, melted

Mix pumpkin, evaporated milk, sugar, eggs, and cinnamon together. Pour into 9 × 13 pan lined with waxed paper. Pour 1 box cake mix (dry) over pumpkin mixture and pat nuts on cake mix. Spoon melted butter evenly over nuts. Bake at 350°F for 50 to 60 minutes. Invert onto tray and peel off waxed paper. When slightly cooled, spread frosting over.

Frosting:
1 package cream cheese (8-oz.), room temperature
1/2 cup powdered sugar, sifted
3/4 cup Cool Whip®

Beat together cream cheese and powdered sugar. Fold in Cool Whip®. Spread over cake evenly. Refrigerate. Cut into squares.

Note: My son-in-law's favorite at Thanksgiving, but a great dessert any time of the year.

Pineapple Upside-Down Cake

yield: 24–30 servings

* *

1/2 cup butter (1 block)
1 cup brown sugar
1 can crushed pineapple, drained (30-oz.)
1 box yellow cake mix

Preheat oven to 350°F. Melt butter in 9×13 pan. Sprinkle brown sugar evenly in pan. Drain fruit. Arrange on sugar mixture.

In large bowl, combine cake mix with 1-1/3 cups water and 2 eggs. Do not substitute fruit juice for water. Blend until moistened and beat at medium speed for 2 minutes. Pour batter over pineapple in pan and bake immediately for about 50 minutes. Let stand 10 to 15 minutes to set. Invert on rectangle platter.

Arare Cookie Crunch

yield: 5 dozen cookies

* *

3/4 cup butter
3/4 cup margarine
1-1/2 cups powdered sugar
2-2/3 cups flour
1-1/2 teaspoons vanilla
2 cups crushed arare (Japanese rice crackers)

In large bowl, beat butter, margarine, and sugar. Add flour and vanilla; mix well. Stir in arare. Drop dough by teaspoonfuls onto ungreased baking sheets and flatten slightly. Bake at 325°F for 20 minutes or until golden brown.

Note: A local favorite with Hawai'i's keiki.

Moist Banana Cake

yield: 24–30 servings

* *

1 cup milk
1 Tablespoon vinegar
1 box yellow cake mix
1 box instant vanilla pudding (3-oz.)
1 teaspoon baking soda
2 to 3 bananas, mashed
1/2 cup oil
4 eggs
1 teaspoon vanilla
1 teaspoon banana extract (optional)
1 cup walnuts, chopped

Mix together milk and vinegar and let stand 5 minutes. Combine cake mix, instant pudding, baking soda, and mashed banana. Blend together with oil, eggs, vanilla, banana extract, and milk and vinegar mixture. Mix in walnuts. Pour into lightly greased 9 × 13 pan. Bake at 350°F for 45 minutes to 1 hour.

Note: An original recipe from my sister-in law, Evie. It is her family's favorite banana cake recipe because it is so moist.

Chocolate Delight

yield: 24 – 30 servings

* *

Crust:
1-1/2 cups flour
3/4 cup butter or margarine (1-1/2 blocks)
1/2 cup walnuts or macadamia nuts, chopped

Blend flour and butter with pastry blender. Mix in nuts. Press lightly into 9 × 13 pan. Bake at 425°F for 10 minutes. Cool.

First Layer:
1 package cream cheese (8-oz.)
1 cup powdered sugar
1/2 container Cool Whip® (half of 12-oz. container)

Beat cream cheese and sugar; mix in Cool Whip® and pour onto cooled crust.

Second Layer:
3 boxes instant chocolate pudding (3-oz. each)
4-1/2 cups cold milk

Combine chocolate pudding and milk, and beat with wire whisk or electric mixer on lowest speed until thick. Pour over first layer.

Topping:
1/2 container Cool Whip®

Top with other half of Cool Whip®. Refrigerate for several hours to set before serving.

Variation: For the second layer, substitute 3 cups milk, 2 boxes of coffee instant-pudding mix, and 1 teaspoon vanilla.

Fresh Mango Pie

yield: 24–30 servings

* *

Crust:
2 cups sifted flour
1 cup butter or margarine (2 blocks)
1/2 cup walnuts, chopped

Cut butter into flour until mixture clings together. Add nuts. Press into 9×13 pan. Bake at 350°F for 20 to 25 minutes. Cool.

Cream Cheese Filling:
1 package cream cheese (8-oz.)
1/2 cup powdered sugar
1 teaspoon vanilla
1 container Cool Whip® (8-oz.)

Mix cream cheese and sugar well; add vanilla. Fold mixture into Cool Whip®. Pour over crust. Refrigerate.

Topping:
2 envelopes Knox® gelatin
1 cup cold water
1 cup boiling water
1 cup sugar, or less
1/4 teaspoon salt
4 Tablespoons lemon juice
yellow food coloring, 2 to 3 drops
4 to 5 cups firm, ripe mangoes, chopped (about 8 Hayden mangoes)

Sprinkle gelatin over 1 cup cold water to soften. Add boiling water, sugar, and salt; stir until thoroughly dissolved. Add lemon juice and food coloring; stir to combine. Cool. Add mangoes and chill until gelatin begins to mold. Spoon over cream cheese filling. Refrigerate until firm.

Banana Cream Delight

yield: 24 servings

* *

Crust:
2 cups flour
1 cup butter or margarine (2 blocks)
1 cup macadamia nuts, chopped fine

Blend flour and butter with pastry blender. Mix in 3/4 cup of the nuts, reserving 1/4 cup to sprinkle. Press into 9 × 13 pan. Bake at 350°F for 25 minutes, or until golden brown. Cool.

Middle Layer:
1 package cream cheese (8-oz.)
1 cup powdered sugar
1/2 container of Cool Whip® (half of 12-oz.)
4 to 5 bananas

Beat cream cheese and powdered sugar until blended and smooth. Mix in Cool Whip®. Spread over cooled crust. Slice bananas evenly over cream cheese layer.

Top Layer:
2 packages instant vanilla pudding (3-oz. each)
3 cups cold milk
remaining Cool Whip®

Whip pudding with milk and spread over bananas. Be sure to seal all edges. Spread remaining Cool Whip® on top. Sprinkle with reserved macadamia nuts. Refrigerate. Chill several hours to set before serving.

Note: Outstanding! My all-time favorite.

Lemon Meringue Pie

yield: 8 servings

* *

1 baked pie shell (9-inch)
1-3/4 cups sugar
1/4 cup cornstarch
3 Tablespoons flour
1/4 teaspoon salt
2 cups water
4 egg yolks, slightly beaten
1/3 cup lemon juice (about 2 lemons)
grated rind of 2 lemons
1 Tablespoon butter

Combine dry ingredients in medium saucepan. Add water slowly, stirring constantly. Cook on medium heat until thick. Quickly stir some of the hot mixture into egg yolks. Pour back into hot mixture, stir to blend. Add lemon juice and rind and continue cooking 2 minutes or more until thick and smooth. Add butter and blend. Cool, stirring occasionally. Pour into baked pie shell. Set aside. Preheat oven to 325°F.

Meringue:
4 egg whites
1/4 teaspoon cream of tartar
1/2 cup sugar

Beat egg whites and cream of tartar at medium speed until frothy. Gradually beat in sugar, beating well after each addition of sugar. Beat at high speed until stiff peaks form when beater is turned off and slowly raised. Spread meringue on pie, carefully sealing to edge of crust. Bake at 325°F for 15 minutes. Cool completely on rack for 2 to 3 hours. Refrigerate, cut with wet knife.

Okinawan Sweet Potato Pie with Haupia Topping

yield: 24–30 servings

* *

Crust:
3/4 cup butter or margarine (1-1/2 blocks)
4 Tablespoons sugar
1-1/2 cups flour
1/2 cup nuts, chopped (optional)

Combine sugar, flour, and nuts. Cut butter into flour mixture until texture is sandy. Press lightly into 9 × 13 pan. Bake at 325°F for 20 to 25 minutes.

Filling:
8 Tablespoons butter or margarine, softened
1 cup sugar
2 eggs, beaten
2 cups Okinawan sweet potato, cooked and mashed
1/2 cup evaporated milk
1 teaspoon vanilla
1/4 teaspoon salt

Beat butter and sugar. Add eggs and mix. Gradually mix in mashed sweet potatoes. Add evaporated milk, vanilla, and salt; mix well. Pour onto crust. Bake at 350°F for 30 to 35 minutes. Cool.

Haupia topping:
1/2 cup sugar
1/2 cup cornstarch
1-1/2 cups water
2 cans frozen coconut milk (12-oz. each), thawed

Combine sugar and cornstarch; stir in water and blend well. Stir sugar mixture into coconut milk; cook and stir over low heat until thickened. Cool slightly. Pour coconut-milk mixture (haupia) over pie filling and refrigerate.

Note: A new favorite that combines the different textures of a light crust, dense sweet potato, and smooth haupia. A hands-down winner at any gathering.

No-Fail Pie Crust

yield: 1 pie crust

* *

1-1/2 cups flour
1/2 teaspoon salt
1-1/2 teaspoons sugar
2 Tablespoons milk
1/2 cup oil

Put ingredients in bowl; use hand to mix all ingredients to a soft dough. Press firmly against sides and bottom of 9-inch pie pan and slightly above. Prick here and there. Bake at 400°F for 10 to 15 minutes until light brown.

Variation: Add chopped macadamia nuts to crust.

Suggestion: Double recipe for 9 × 13 pan. Use for any instant pudding pie mix or even as a crust for Quiche Lorraine.

Shortbread Cookies

yield: 24 – 30 servings

* *

1 cup butter or margarine (2 blocks)
1/2 cup sugar
1 teaspoon vanilla
2 cups flour

Beat together butter and sugar until light and fluffy. Add vanilla. Mix in flour. Pat into 9 × 13 pan and prick with fork. Bake at 325°F for 35 to 40 minutes or until golden in color. Cut into squares while still warm.

Tofu Pie

yield: 8 servings

* *

1 Keebler® Ready Crust® (butter pie crust or graham)
1 package lemon Jell-O® (3-oz.)
1 cup boiling water
1 to 2 Tablespoons lemon juice
1/2 teaspoon lemon extract
1/2 of 20-oz. tofu, smooth/soft type
1/2 container Cool Whip® (half of 8-oz.)

Mix together Jell-O®, boiling water, lemon juice, and lemon extract. Refrigerate until slightly firm. Drain tofu. Blend tofu and Cool Whip® in Osterizer® or use electric mixer. Mix in Jell-O® mixture. Pour into crust and refrigerate. When firm, garnish with kiwi fruit or any canned fruit.

Variation: Substitute strawberry Jell-O® for lemon Jell-O®. Garnish with sliced fresh strawberries.

Note: You must try this! Tofu is blended and mixed and transformed into a smooth refreshing dessert. No one will know it's tofu. My daughter, Cheryl, always raves about this pie.

Pumpkin Custard Pie

yield: 30 servings

* *

Crust:
3 cups flour
1 Tablespoon sugar
1 cup oil
1 teaspoon salt
4 Tablespoons milk

Combine ingredients in large bowl and mix together well. Press firmly into 9 × 13 pan. Prick bottom and bake at 400°F for 20 minutes, until light brown. Cool.

Pudding Layer:
2 boxes instant vanilla pudding mix (3-oz. each)
2-1/2 cups milk

Beat together pudding mix and milk on medium speed. (Do not place on crust at this time.) Refrigerate until set, about 15 minutes.

Pumpkin Mixture:
4 eggs, slightly beaten
1 can pumpkin (29-oz.)
1 teaspoon salt
2 teaspoons cinnamon
2 cans sweetened condensed milk (14-oz. each)
1/2 cup water
1/2 cup sugar
1 teaspoon ground ginger
1/2 teaspoon ground cloves

Mix together all ingredients until well blended.

Pour prepared pudding on cooled crust. Spoon pumpkin mixture onto pudding mix. Bake at 425°F for 15 minutes. Reduce temperature to 350°F and bake for 40 to 50 minutes, or until done. Cool.

Note: Pie will still be soft, so be careful when taking it out of oven. Cool for several hours to set. Need not be refrigerated.

Haupia Chocolate Pie

yield: 24–30 servings

* *

Crust:
2 cups graham crackers, crushed (about 24 crackers)
1 cup butter, melted (2 blocks)

Grind or crush graham crackers into crumbs. Mix with melted butter and press into 9 × 13 pan. Refrigerate.

Haupia:
3 cans frozen coconut milk, thawed (12-oz. each)
1-1/4 cups sugar
1-1/4 cups cornstarch

In a pot, mix all ingredients until smooth. Cook on medium heat, stirring continuously, until mixture thickens. Spread over crust. Refrigerate.

Chocolate Topping:
3 boxes cook-and-serve chocolate pudding
4-1/2 cups milk

Combine pudding mix and milk and cook on medium heat, stirring continuously until thick and bubbles appear. Remove from heat and cool slightly while continuing to mix so film doesn't form at top. Spread pudding over haupia. Refrigerate.

Note: The best! Everyone raves about this pie. It takes a little effort but it's worth it.

Kona Coffee Mud Pie

yield: 24 servings

* *

1 pound package Oreo® cookies (about 40 cookies)
3/4 cup butter, melted
1/2 cup nuts, chopped fine
1/2 gallon Kona coffee ice cream
1 container Cool Whip® (8-oz.)
macadamia nuts, chopped fine, for sprinkling

Put cookies in plastic bag and roll to make crumbs. Put crumbs in bowl. Add butter and nuts and mix well. Press crumbs into 9×13 pan and bake at 400°F for 8 minutes. Cool well.

Cut the ice cream into fourths and press on cooled crumbs. Spread Cool Whip® over ice cream. Sprinkle with macadamia nuts. Freeze.

Variation: Use 2 flavors of ice cream. Instead of baking crust, leave it unbaked.

Note: Kelsie Kodama loves this pie. Thank you to her mom, Raynette—my dental hygienist—who shared this recipe with me.

Blueberry Cream Cheese Pie

yield: 24 – 30 servings

* *

Crust:
3/4 cup butter (1-1/2 blocks)
1/2 cup brown sugar
1-1/2 cups flour
1 cup nuts, chopped

> Beat butter and brown sugar; add flour and nuts. Press dough into buttered 9 × 13 pan. Bake at 375°F for 10 minutes or until top browns. Cool.

Filling:
2 packages cream cheese (8-oz. each)
1 cup powdered sugar, sifted
2 teaspoons vanilla
2 containers Cool Whip® (8-oz. each)
1 can blueberry pie filling (21-oz.)

> Beat together cream cheese, powdered sugar, and vanilla. Add Cool Whip® and fold into cream cheese mixture. Pour on crust evenly. Top with blueberry pie filling. Chill for several hours to set before serving.

Irresistible
Peanut Butter Cookies

yield: 3 dozen

* *

3/4 cup creamy peanut butter
1/2 cup Crisco® shortening
1-1/4 cups light brown sugar, firmly packed
3 Tablespoons milk
1 Tablespoon vanilla
1 egg
1-3/4 cups flour
3/4 teaspoon salt
3/4 teaspoon baking soda

In large bowl, combine peanut butter, shortening, sugar, milk, and vanilla. Beat at medium speed until well blended. Add egg. Beat just until blended.

Combine flour, salt, and baking soda. Add to creamed mixture at low speed. Mix just until blended. Drop by heaping teaspoonfuls 2 inches apart onto ungreased baking sheet. Flatten slightly in crisscross pattern with tines of fork. Bake at 375°F for 7 to 8 minutes, or until just beginning to brown. Cool 2 minutes on baking sheet. Remove cookies and place on sheet of foil to cool completely.

Sponge Drops
yield: 5 dozen cookies

* *

3 eggs
3/4 cup sugar
1/2 teaspoon cream of tartar
1/4 teaspoon baking soda
1 cup plus 2 Tablespoons cake flour, sifted
parchment paper for cookie sheet

Beat eggs well, until fluffy and light. Add sugar slowly and continue beating. In another bowl, combine sifted flour, baking soda, and cream of tartar and sift again. Add into egg mixture and beat well. Let set for 15 to 20 minutes. Drop dough from teaspoon on parchment-lined cookie sheet and bake at 350°F to 375°F for about 5 minutes, or until brown. Cool slightly on parchment paper. Use spatula to transfer cookies to cooling rack. Refrigerate. Bake cookies 1 day before adding whipped cream. Refrigerate in covered container. Layer with waxed paper to prevent any sticking.

Whipped Cream:
2 Tablespoons powdered sugar
1 teaspoon vanilla
1 cup whipping cream

Beat together sugar, vanilla, and cream until whipped. Sprinkle powdered sugar on cookies. Top cookies with whipped cream or place two cookies together with whipped cream in the middle.

Note: When I asked Roberta Tokumaru, 'Aikahi Elementary School's principal, for her favorite dessert, she replied, "Sponge Drops." I taste-tested it and everyone loved it! It is a little challenging when preparing it for the first time, but it gets easier.

Sugar Cookies

yield: 30 pieces

* *

1-1/2 cups sifted powdered sugar
1 cup butter
1 egg
1 teaspoon vanilla
1/2 teaspoon almond extract
2-1/2 cups flour, sifted
1 teaspoon cream of tartar
1 teaspoon baking soda

Beat sugar and butter; add egg, vanilla, and almond extract. Mix thoroughly. Sift flour, cream of tartar, and baking soda. Stir into butter mixture and blend together. Refrigerate 2 to 3 hours. Divide dough in half and roll out on lightly floured board. Roll thin but thick enough to pick up the design of the cookie cutters. Dip cutter in flour before each rolling. Cut as many cookies from each rolling as possible. The least amount of working with the dough gives the best cookie. Place on lightly greased baking sheet. Bake at 375°F for 7 to 8 minutes or until delicately golden.

Furikake Chex® Mix

yield: about 11 quarts

* *

3 boxes Crispix® (12-oz. each), or use Rice Chex® and Corn
  Chex® to equal 36-oz.
1 jar aji nori furikake (1.3-oz.)
1 jar unsalted dry roasted peanuts (12-oz.)
2 packages premium mixed arare (Enjoy® brand), (8-oz. each
  or about 6 cups)
1 package lightly salted macadamia nuts (12-oz.)
1 can cashew halves with pieces (9.25-oz.)

Sauce:
1/2 cup butter (1 block)
3/8 cup sugar
2 Tablespoons soy sauce
1/2 cup vegetable oil
1/2 cup Karo® Light Corn Syrup

In small saucepan slowly melt butter on low heat. Add sugar
and soy sauce and heat until sugar is dissolved. Turn off heat
and add oil and corn syrup. Set aside to cool.

Place cereal in very large aluminum pan (or divide cereal into
2 large pans). Slowly drizzle the "almost cool" sauce mixture
over cereal, a little at a time, and toss to coat. Sprinkle
furikake and toss gently. Add nuts and arare; toss. Bake at
250°F for 1 hour. Mix every 15 minutes.

Variation: Substitute other combinations of nuts and arare
of your choice.

*Note: Ever since my sister-in-law Amy shared this great
tasting local Chex® mix with us last Christmas, it has
become our favorite.*

Lemon Bars

yield: 24 – 36 bars

* *

Crust:
1-1/2 cups flour
1/2 cup powdered sugar
3/4 cup butter or margarine (1-1/2 blocks)

Combine flour and powdered sugar; cut in butter until crumbly. Press onto bottom of lightly greased 9×13 pan. Bake at 350°F for 25 to 30 minutes or until golden brown.

Topping:
4 eggs, slightly beaten
1-1/2 cups sugar
1 teaspoon baking powder
3 Tablespoons flour
1/2 cup lemon juice (about 5 lemons)

While crust is baking, combine topping ingredients and mix well. Pour over baked crust (no need to let crust cool) and return to oven. Bake 20 to 25 minutes or until golden brown. Cool. Cut into bars. Sprinkle with powdered sugar. Store in refrigerator.

Variation: Substitute the 1/2 cup lemon juice with about 10 Tablespoons fresh liliko'i juice and 1/4 teaspoon lemon juice to produce fantastic tart and tangy liliko'i bars. This is suggested by my oncologist Dr. Clayton Chong.

Hawaiian Chocolate Chip Cookies

yield: 3 dozen large cookies

* *

1 cup shortening
3/4 cup sugar
3/4 cup brown sugar
1 egg
1 teaspoon vanilla
1-1/2 cups flour
1 teaspoon baking powder
1 teaspoon baking soda
1/8 teaspoon salt
2 cups quick oats
1 cup semisweet chocolate chips
1 cup macadamia nuts, chopped
1 cup shredded coconut

Beat shortening and sugars until light and fluffy. Add egg and vanilla; beat well. Sift flour, baking powder, soda, and salt; gradually mix into shortening and sugar mixture. Stir in remaining ingredients. Shape into 1-1/2-inch balls and place on ungreased cookie sheets. Flatten with bottom of glass dipped in flour. Bake at 325°F for 15 minutes or until lightly browned.

Note: It's easy to prepare and has everything to make this a great cookie.

Old-Fashioned Oatmeal Cookies

yield: 6-7 dozen

* *

1 cup raisins
1 cup water
3/4 cup shortening
1-1/2 cups sugar
2 eggs
1 teaspoon vanilla
2-1/2 cups flour
1/2 teaspoon baking powder
1 teaspoon soda
1 teaspoon salt
1 teaspoon cinnamon
1/2 teaspoon cloves
2 cups rolled oats
1/2 cup nuts, chopped

Simmer raisins and water in saucepan over low heat (20 to 30 minutes). Drain raisin liquid into measuring cup. Add enough water to make 1/2 cup. In large bowl, mix shortening, sugar, eggs, and vanilla. Stir in raisin liquid.

Stir together flour, baking powder, soda, salt, and spices; blend in raisin liquid mixture. Add rolled oats, nuts, and raisins. Drop rounded teaspoonfuls of dough about 2-inches apart on ungreased baking sheet. Bake at 400°F for 8 to 10 minutes or until lightly browned.

Almond Cookies
yield: 5-1/2 dozen

* *

1 cup plus 3 Tablespoons shortening or butter
1 cup sugar
1 egg, beaten
1 teaspoon almond extract
2-1/2 cups flour
1/2 teaspoon salt
1/2 teaspoon baking soda
red food color
almonds, blanched (optional)

Beat shortening and sugar; add egg and almond extract. Mix well. Sift flour, salt, and baking soda; add to sugar and egg mixture. Mix well. Shape into walnut-size balls. Place on ungreased cookie sheet. Using thumb, press center of balls to make a depression. Using the end of a chopstick, dip in red food color and place a dot in the center of each cookie. A blanched almond may be pressed into the center if preferred. Bake at 350°F for 15 to 18 minutes.

Note: This is an authentic Chinese almond cookie recipe that was shared by Aunty Clara (Chun). The best almond cookie recipe I have tasted.

Andagi

yield: 4 dozen

* *

5 cups flour
2 cups sugar
7 teaspoons baking powder
1/4 teaspoon salt
5 eggs, beaten
1/3 cup Wesson® oil
1-1/2 cups water, more or less
Oil for deep-frying

Sift together flour, sugar, baking powder, and salt in large bowl. In small bowl, beat 5 eggs and mix together with oil. Pour egg mixture into the dry ingredients. Add water, starting with 1 cup and adding just enough to completely moisten. DO NOT OVERMIX. Drop by tablespoon, using a teaspoon to scrape batter off tablespoon into hot oil (350°F to 365°F) and cook 3 to 5 minutes, or until nice and brown.* Do not crowd the andagi. They will roll around by themselves. Drain on paper towels. Test doneness by inserting a skewer through doughnut.

Hint: The next day, any leftover andagi can be placed in toaster oven at 350°F for about 15 minutes.

*I begin on medium heat on stove top and adjust heat as necessary.

Note: This is the well-known Hilo andagi recipe. Easy for beginners and very tasty.

Almond Float

yield: 6–8 servings

* *

1-1/2 envelopes unflavored gelatin
1/2 cup evaporated milk
1-1/2 cups water, divided
1/2 cup sugar (or less)
2 teaspoons almond extract
fruit (mandarin oranges, lychee, fruit cocktail, etc.)

Dissolve gelatin in 1/2 cup of the water. Heat evaporated milk, 1 cup of the water, and sugar to just below boiling point; add gelatin mixture. Stir until sugar and gelatin are completely dissolved. Cool; add almond extract. Pour into 8-inch square pan or mold. Refrigerate to set. Cut into cube pieces and serve with desired fruits.

Blueberry Mochi

yield: 24–30 servings

* *

1 pound mochiko (16-oz. box)
1 cup butter, melted
2 cups sugar
1 can evaporated milk (12-oz.)
4 eggs
2 teaspoons baking powder
2 teaspoons vanilla
1 can blueberry pie filling

Stir sugar in melted butter. Add milk and mix well. Add eggs and mix. Stir in baking powder, mochiko, and vanilla. Pour into ungreased 9 × 13 pan. Fold in the blueberry pie filling creating a marbleized look. Bake at 350°F for 1 hour or until toothpick tests clean.

Goodie Goodie Dessert

yield: 12–16 servings

* *

2 cans 7 Up®
4 cans strawberry soda
1 can evaporated milk (12-oz.)
1 can sweetened condensed milk (14-oz.)

Mix all ingredients with whisk and blend well. Pour in deep plastic container with cover. Freeze for 5 hours. Mix again with fork. Re-freeze.

King's Hawaiian®
Sweet Bread–Bread Pudding

yield: 9 × 13 pan

* *

1 King's Hawaiian® **Sweet Bread (16-oz.)**
raisins, cinnamon, nutmeg for sprinkling
3 cups milk
1 cup sugar
1-1/2 cups butter, melted
9 eggs, beaten
1-1/2 teaspoons vanilla

Break bread into large pieces. Place into buttered 9 × 13 pan. Sprinkle raisins, cinnamon, and nutmeg over bread pieces. In saucepan, combine milk, sugar, and butter; heat to boiling point. Remove from heat; add beaten eggs. (Be careful that milk mixture is not so hot that it could curdle eggs.) Add vanilla; mix and pour over bread, making sure bread is soaked. Sprinkle more cinnamon and nutmeg over pudding, if desired. Bake at 350°F for 20 to 25 minutes or until knife inserted in middle of pudding comes out clean.

Rainbow Finger Jell-O®

yield: 24–30 servings

* *

**4 packages Jell-O® (3-oz. each): 1 each strawberry, lemon,
lime, orange
6 envelopes Knox® unflavored gelatin
1 cup Eagle Brand® sweetened condensed milk
Hot water**

Combine strawberry Jell-O®, 1 envelope Knox® gelatin, and
1-1/2 cup hot water. Cool. Pour into 9 × 13 pan greased with
mayonnaise. Place in refrigerator to set, about 30 minutes.

Mix 1 cup condensed milk with 1 cup hot water. Set aside.
Mix 2 envelopes Knox® gelatin with 1 cup hot water; combine with milk mixture.

Pour about 1 cup of the milk mixture for the next layer.
Refrigerate to set. (Each layer will now set quickly, about 15
minutes each.)

Combine lemon Jell-O®, 1 envelope Knox® gelatin, and 1-1/2
cup hot water. Cool. Pour carefully over milk mixture; place
in refrigerator to set.

Repeat, using lime and ending with orange Jell-O®, with milk
layer between Jell-O® layers.

Hint: Be sure pan used is even, so the layers are even.

Variation: Substitute any flavor Jell-O®.

Tri-Colored Mochi

yield: 9 × 13 pan

* *

1 pound mochiko (16-oz. box)
2 cups sugar
1 teaspoon baking powder
1 can coconut milk (12-oz.)
2 cups water
1 teaspoon vanilla
food coloring, red and green
katakuriko (potato starch) for dusting

In a large mixing bowl combine mochiko, sugar, and baking powder. Blend water, coconut milk, and vanilla. Add to dry ingredients gradually, mixing thoroughly with whisk or spoon.

Remove 2 cups of mixture. Add about 3 drops of green coloring. Pour into greased 9 × 13 pan. Cover with foil and bake 15 minutes at 350°F.

Pour 2 cups white mixture over first layer. Cover with foil and bake 20 minutes.

Add red coloring to remaining mixture and pour over second layer. Cover and bake for 30 minutes. Cool uncovered, preferably overnight. Cover with clean dishcloth. Cut with plastic knife when mochi is totally cooled. Coat with potato starch.

Hint: Lessen water by 1/2 or 1/4 cup if firmer mochi is desired. If water is lessened, measure slightly less than 2 cups for each layer.

Note: I make this for Girl's Day. Very colorful. Pieces may be individually wrapped with waxed paper.

Moist Chocolate Cake

yield: 24 servings

* *

2 cups all-purpose flour
1 teaspoon salt
1 teaspoon baking powder
2 teaspoons baking soda
3/4 cup unsweetened cocoa
2 cups sugar
1 cup vegetable oil
1 cup hot coffee
1 cup milk
2 eggs
1 teaspoon vanilla extract

Sift together all dry ingredients. Add oil, coffee, and milk; mix at medium speed for 2 minutes. Add eggs and vanilla; beat 2 more minutes. Pour into 2 greased and floured 9-inch cake pans. Bake at 325°F for 25 to 30 minutes.

Icing:
1 cup milk
5 Tablespoons all-purpose flour
1/2 cup butter, softened at room temperature
1/2 cup shortening
1 cup sugar
1 teaspoon vanilla extract

Combine milk and flour in saucepan; cook until thick. Cover and refrigerate. In a medium mixing bowl, beat butter, shortening, sugar, and vanilla until creamy. Add chilled milk and flour mixture and beat for 10 minutes. Frost cooled cake.

Note: Pearl Nakamura, my cousin in Hilo, brought this fabulous chocolate cake to a family get-together. She is often asked for the recipe. (I've also used a 9 × 13 pan. Bake at 325°F for 45 minutes.)

Broken Glass Dessert

yield: 24 servings

* *

4 packages Jell-O® (3-oz. each): 1 each strawberry, lemon, lime, orange
4 cups hot water
1 quart skim milk
5 envelopes Knox® unflavored gelatin
1 cup sugar

Note: Prepare Jell-O® a day earlier. Dissolve each Jell-O® separately in 1 cup hot water. Cool and refrigerate overnight.

The next day, combine skim milk, gelatin, and sugar in saucepan. Heat to dissolve sugar and gelatin. Pour into large container. Cool to room temperature. Cut Jell-O® into approximately 3/4-inch cubes; fold into milk mixture. Pour into 9 × 13 pan. Refrigerate about 3 to 4 hours to firmly set.

Coconut Butter Mochi

yield: 24 servings

* *

1 box mochiko (16-oz.)
1-3/4 cups sugar
2 teaspoons baking powder
1/2 cup butter (1 block), melted
5 eggs
2 cups milk
1 can coconut milk (12-oz.)
1/2 teaspoon vanilla extract
1/2 teaspoon coconut extract
1 cup Baker's® Angel Flakes Coconut (set aside 1/4 cup to
 sprinkle over top for the last 10 to 15 minutes of baking.)

In large mixing bowl, combine mochiko, sugar, and baking
powder. In separate bowl, mix together rest of ingredients.
Add to dry ingredients and mix well. Pour into greased or
buttered 9 × 13 pan. Bake at 350°F for 45 minutes or until
toothpick inserted comes out clean. (Sprinkle reserved coconut flakes the last 15 minutes of baking.)

*Note: My mother tasted this yummy mochi at a party about
three years ago and kept talking about how good it tasted.
She finally got the recipe thanks to Rose Watanabe. The
mochi is moist and almost like a bread pudding texture!*

Fruitcake Bars

yield: 30 bars

* *

Crust:
1-1/2 cups flour
1/3 cup sugar
3/4 cup butter

Mix until crumbly. Press into lightly greased 9×13 pan. Bake at 350°F for about 10 minutes or until light brown.

Topping:
1/2 cup sifted flour
1 teaspoon baking powder
1/4 teaspoon salt
4 eggs, slightly beaten
1 cup sugar
1 teaspoon vanilla
1 cup candied fruit, chopped
1 cup chopped nuts

Sift flour, baking powder, and salt together; set aside. Mix sugar with eggs and vanilla. Toss fruit and nuts in flour and add to egg mixture. Pour over baked crust and bake at 350°F for 20 to 25 minutes. Cut into bars while still warm; sprinkle with powdered sugar.

Note: At my first mochi book signing in 2000, Jean Machida Bart, my '57 Hilo High classmate, showed up with a gift of cookies to congratulate me. I was so happy and grateful to see her. I especially loved her fruitcake bars. I had to include her recipe for others to enjoy.

Melt 'em Cookies
yield: 6-1/2 dozen

* *

1 cup butter (2 blocks), softened to room temperature
1 cup Wesson® oil or Crisco®
1 cup white sugar
1 cup powdered sugar
2 eggs
1 teaspoon vanilla
4-1/4 cups flour
1 teaspoon salt
1 teaspoon cream of tartar
1 teaspoon baking soda

Beat butter and oil with white and powdered sugar until smooth. Add eggs and vanilla; beat until well blended. Sift dry ingredients and add into butter mixture. Mix well. Scoop out a heaping teaspoonful of batter and place on ungreased cookie sheet. Batter will be soft. Press bottom of a glass on granulated sugar; then press down on round balls of batter to flatten. Bake at 350°F for 10 minutes.

Note: You must try this recipe! The cookies are so light, thin, and crispy. I got this recipe from Evelyn Shiraki who makes wonderful cookies, and she got it from Jeanette Akamichi many, many years ago when we all worked together at Pū'ōhala Elementary school.

Energy Bars with Fruits

yield: 96 pieces

✳ ✳

Dried fruits:
1/3 cup raisins
1/3 cup golden raisins
1/3 cup cranberries
8 dates, chopped and floured in 1 Tablespoon flour
  (use sieve to remove excess flour)
6 apricot halves, chopped
1 pear half, chopped
1 peach half, chopped

1 cup toasted sesame seeds
1-1/4 cups dry roasted peanuts, unsalted
1 pound 2-oz. Quick 1 Minute Quaker® Oats (6 cups)
1/8 teaspoon salt
7 cups Rice Krispies®
1/2 cup creamy peanut butter
1/4 cup butter (half block), softened
1 pound large marshmallows

Grease 9×13 pan; set aside. In large microwaveable bowl, blend peanut butter and softened butter together thoroughly; set aside.

In large skillet, toast oatmeal on medium-low about 15 to 30 minutes, sprinkling salt over. Stir cereal every five minutes. Heat until very warm to the palm of your hand. Add fruits, nuts, and sesame seeds. Mix thoroughly. Add Rice Krispies®; mix carefully and heat until very warm to palm of hand. Continue to keep oatmeal mixture warm on stove.

Place marshmallows on top of peanut butter mixture and microwave for 1 minute 13 seconds. (While microwaving marshmallows, place warm oatmeal mixture in very large container.) Remove bowl from microwave and work quickly to blend marshmallows and peanut butter. Add to warm oatmeal mixture and stir quickly and gently until the marshmallow mixture coats all the dry ingredients. Place mixture in pan.

With buttered fingers (or use foil or waxed paper) press mixture evenly in pan. Use another pan to help press mixture evenly. Cool. Cut into bars. Wrap in waxed paper. Need not refrigerate if consumed within one month.

Suggestion: To cut bars, first cut out a piece measuring 2 × 9-inches. Place on cutting board and cut in half, then half again, and so on until you have 16 pieces measuring 1 × 2-inches each. Do that five more times and you will have 96 pieces.

Variation: The amount of chopped dried fruits should total 1-1/2 cups. You could omit the pear half and peach half and substitute with other dried fruit.

Note: The first time I made this it was a little difficult. Since then I've made these energy bars many times and it has gotten easier. These energy bars are the lightest and best of all that I have ever made. I have had many requests for the recipe. They are great to take along on long trips away from home.

Zucchini Cake

yield: 24 servings

* *

2-1/2 cups flour
1-3/4 cups sugar
1-1/2 teaspoons cinnamon
1 teaspoon salt
1/2 teaspoon baking powder
1/2 teaspoon baking soda
4 eggs, beaten
1 cup vegetable oil
2 cups zucchini, shredded (about 1 large zucchini)
1/2 cup macadamia nuts or walnuts, chopped

Frosting:
3 oz. cream cheese, softened
1/4 cup butter, softened
1 Tablespoon milk
1 teaspoon vanilla
1-3/4 cups powdered sugar

Combine flour, sugar, cinnamon, salt, baking powder, and baking soda in mixing bowl. Combine eggs and oil; add to dry ingredients and mix well. Add zucchini and stir until thoroughly combined. Fold in nuts. Pour into greased 9 × 13 pan. Bake at 350°F for 35 to 40 minutes or until a toothpick inserted near center comes out clean. Cool.

For frosting, beat cream cheese, butter, milk, and vanilla in small bowl until smooth. Add powdered sugar and mix well. Frost cake. (Sprinkle with finely chopped nuts if desired.) Store in refrigerator.

Note: This zucchini cake is really good! It was recommended to me by Avolia Olson in Hilo and everyone who has tasted it likes it. The cake is not very sweet and the cream cheese frosting is a perfect match for it.

Glossary

* *

aburage	deep fried tofu, fried bean curd
adobo	vinegar-flavored meat
'ahi	yellowfin tuna
araimo dasheen	Japanese taro
black beans	salted and fermented black beans
Chinese parsley	cilantro
choi sum	Chinese broccoli
chung choi	(or chung choy) preserved salted turnip
daikon	white radish or turnip
dau see	salted and fermented black beans
fueru wakame	dehydrated seaweed
furikake	rice condiment made with seaweed flakes
gau gee	Chinese dumpling, usually deep-fried
gobo	burdock root
harm ha	shrimp sauce
haupia	coconut cornstarch pudding
Hawaiian salt	coarse sea salt
'inamona	roasted, pounded, and salted kukui nut
iriko	small dried fish
jook	rice soup
kamaboko	fish cake
kim chee	hot, spicy preserved vegetable
kinpira gobo	burdock root stir-fried with soy sauce and sugar
konbu	dried seaweed, dried kelp
konyaku	tuber root flour cake
laulau	steamed bundle of meat in ti leaves
limu	seaweed
long rice	translucent mung bean noodles
lū'au leaves	taro leaves
lumpia	spring roll filled with meat, vegetables, or fruit
lumpia wrapper	thin flour wrappers for fried rolls
mirin	sweet rice wine
miso	fermented soybean paste
mochiko	glutinous rice flour

nishime	cooked vegetable dish
nishime kombu	narrow kelp used in nishime
ocean salad	deep-sea seasoned seaweed
ong choy	swamp spinach or cabbage
'ōpakapaka	pink snapper
oyster sauce	oyster flavored sauce
panko	flour meal for breading
patis	clear fish sauce
sake	rice wine
shiitake	mushrooms
shoyu	soy sauce
somen	fine wheat flour noodles
sukiyaki	vegetable and meat dish
teriyaki	soy-based sauce
taegu	spice flavored codfish
ti leaf	broad leaf of ti plant
tofu	fresh soybean curd
tortilla	Mexican flat bread made of cornmeal or wheat flour
udon noodles	Japanese wheat noodles
wasabi	Japanese horseradish, sold in paste and powdered form
won bok	Chinese cabbage, makina, napa
yakitori	Japanese-style grilled chicken

Index

✳ ✳

Symbols

24-Hour Lettuce Salad, 32
7-Layer Dip, 3

A

Aburage,
  Hearty Miso Soup, 50
  Nishime, 39
  Stuffed Aburage with Somen, 18
'Ahi Limu Poke, 2
Almond Float, 147
Andagi, 146
Arare Cookie Crunch, 125

B

Bacardi® Rum Cake, 114
Bacon,
  Baked Beans, 34
  Broccoli Salad, 20
  Country Comfort Corn Chowder, 49
  Oyster Bacon Wrap, 15
  Spinach Salad with Hot Dressing, 27
  Turkey Chowder, 58
Baked Beans, 34
Baked Fish, 99
Bamboo shoots,
  Hot and Sour Soup, 51
  Imitation Bird Nest Soup, 53
  Nishime, 39
Banana Cream Delight, 129
Barbecue Sticks, 7
Bean Salad, 22
Bean sprouts,
  Butter Yaki, 98
  Namul, 38
  Shrimp Lumpia, 16
  Tofu Salad, 30
Beef,
  Barbecue Sticks, 7
  Beef Broccoli, 62

Beef Tomato, 63
Corned Beef Hash Patties, 64
DeLuz Vindha D'Ahlos Roast, 71
Easy Pot Roast, 68
Jumbo's Restaurant's Beef Stew, 65
Lasagna, 69
Laulau, 73
Minestrone Soup, 54
No-Fail Roast Beef, 70
Oxtail Soup, 55
Spanish Rice, 108
Spring Rolls, 9
Stuffed Cabbage Rolls, 67
Sukiyaki, 66
Beef Broccoli, 62
Beef Tomato, 63
Bell pepper,
  Bean Salad, 22
  Beef Tomato, 63
  Broccoli Shrimp Salad, 23
  Cashew Chicken, 84
  Chicken Cacciatore, 83
  Lasagna, 69
  Pasta Salad, 21
Black Bean Soup, 47
Black Bean Spareribs, 76
Blueberry Cream Cheese Pie, 137
Blueberry Mochi, 147
Broccoli Salad, 20
Broccoli Shrimp Salad, 23
Broken Glass Dessert, 152
Buffalo Wings, 10
Butterfish with Shoyu Sauce, 104
Butter Yaki, 98

C

Carrot Cake, 119
Cashew Chicken, 84
Chicken,
  Black Bean Soup, 47
  Buffalo Wings, 10

Butter Yaki, 98
Cashew Chicken, 84
Chicken Adobo, 87
Chicken Cacciatore, 83
Chicken Chili, 85
Chicken Enchilada, 86
Chicken Katsu, 88
Chicken Long Rice, 90
Chinese Chicken Salad, 24
Cold Chicken with Ginger Sauce, 93
Easy Roast Chicken, 95
Flavored Chicken for Chinese Stir-fry, 89
Fried Chicken, 92
Gay's Easy Potluck Chicken, 91
Lemon Chicken, 94
Mochiko Chicken, 96
Mushroom Soup, 46
Nishime, 39
Sesame Chicken, 11
Shoyu Chicken, 95
Yakitori, 91
Chiffon Cake, 116
Chinese cabbage,
    Chinese Cabbage Soup, 48
    Flavored Chicken for Chinese Stir-fry, 89
    'Ōpakapaka with Chinese Cabbage, 101
Chinese Chicken Salad, 24
Chinese Steamed Fish, 102
Chocolate Banana Bread, 112
Chocolate Delight, 127
Choi Sum, 35
Clam Dip, 5
Cocktail Shrimp, 12
Cocoa Cake, 115
Coconut Butter Mochi, 153
Cold Chicken with Ginger Sauce, 93
Corn Bread, 120
Corned Beef Hash Patties, 64
Country Comfort Corn Chowder, 49
Creamsicle Cake, 121
Crispy Gau Gee, 17
Cucumber Namasu, 41
Curry Mango Cream Cheese Spread, 4

D

DeLuz Vindha D'Ahlos Roast, 71

E

Easy Pot Roast, 68
Easy Roast Chicken, 95
Easy Seafood Pasta, 105
Eggplant,
    Sari Sari, 75
Energy Bars with Fruits, 156

F

Flavored Chicken for Chinese Stir-fry, 89
Fresh Mango Pie, 128
Fried Chicken, 92
Fruitcake Bars, 154
Furikake Chex® Mix, 141
Furikake Salmon, 106
Furikake Seared 'Ahi, 13

G

Gay's Easy Potluck Chicken, 91
Gon Lo Mein, 44
Goodie Goodie Dessert, 148
Green bean,
    Bean Salad, 22
    Flavored Chicken for Chinese Stir-fry, 89
    Green Bean Casserole, 36
    Roasted Vegetables, 43
    Sari Sari, 75
    Shrimp Lumpia, 16
Guacamole, 6

H

Haupia Chocolate Pie, 135
Hawaiian Chocolate Chip Cookies, 143
Hearty Miso Soup, 50
Honey Glazed Walnut Shrimp, 100
Hot and Sour Soup, 51

I

Imitation Bird Nest Soup, 53
Irresistible Peanut Butter Cookies, 138

J

Jook (Chinese Rice Porridge), 52
Jumbo's Restaurant's Beef Stew, 65

K

Kahlúa® Cake, 117
Kim Chee Soup, 59
King's Hawaiian® Sweet Bread-
   Bread Pudding, 148
Kinpira Gobo with Portuguese Sausage, 37
Kona Coffee Mud Pie, 136

L

Lamb,
   McCarthy's Marinade, 97
   Roast Lamb, 72
Lasagna, 69
Laulau, 73
Lemon Bars, 142
Lemon Chicken, 94
Lemon Meringue Pie, 130

M

Mandarin Peach Cake, 123
Mango Bread, 118
Ma Po Tofu (Pork Tofu), 82
McCarthy's Marinade, 97
Melt 'em Cookies, 155
Mimi's Shrimp, 14
Minestrone Soup, 54
Miso Butterfish, 99
Miso Pork Roast, 79
Mochiko Chicken, 96
Moist Banana Cake, 126
Moist Chocolate Cake, 151
Mushroom Pork Chops, 80
Mushroom Soup, 46

N

Namul, 38
Nishime, 39
No-Fail Pie Crust, 132
No-Fail Roast Beef, 70

O

Okinawan Sweet Potato Pie
   with Haupia Topping, 131
Old-Fashioned Oatmeal Cookies, 144
Ong Choy and Harm Ha, 40

'Ōpakapaka with Chinese Cabbage, 101
Oriental-Style Fish, 109
Oxtail Soup, 55
Oyster Bacon Wrap, 15

P

Pineapple Upside-Down Cake, 125
Pine Nut Salad, 25
Poppy Seed Bundt Cake, 122
Pork,
   Black Bean Spareribs, 76
   Chinese Cabbage Soup, 48
   Crispy Gau Gee, 17
   Hot and Sour Soup, 51
   Imitation Bird Nest Soup, 53
   Kim Chee Soup, 59
   Lazy-Style Laulau, 73
   Ma Po Tofu (Pork Tofu), 82
   Miso Pork Roast, 79
   Mushroom Pork Chops, 80
   Pork-Tofu Casserole, 81
   Pork Hash, 78
   Roast Pork, 80
   Sari Sari, 75
   Spring Rolls, 9
   Stuffed Cabbage Rolls, 67
   Stuffed Tofu, 110
   Sweet-Sour Spareribs, 77
   Tonkatsu, 74
   Won Ton Soup, 60
Pork-Tofu Casserole, 81
Pork Hash, 78
Portuguese Bean Soup, 56
Potato and Macaroni Salad, 31
Pumpkin Crunch, 124
Pumpkin Custard Pie, 134

R

Rainbow Finger Jell-O®, 149
Roasted Vegetables, 43
Roast Lamb, 72
Roast Pork, 80

S

Sari Sari, 75
Scalloped Potatoes, 34
Seafood,
  'Ahi Limu Poke, 2
  Baked Fish, 99
  Broccoli Shrimp Salad, 23
  Butterfish with Shoyu Sauce, 104
  Chinese Steamed Fish, 102
  Cocktail Shrimp, 12
  Crispy Gau Gee, 17
  Easy Seafood Pasta, 105
  Furikake Salmon, 106
  Honey Glazed Walnut Shrimp, 100
  Mimi's Shrimp, 14
  Miso Butterfish, 99
  'Ōpakapaka with Chinese Cabbage, 101
  Oriental-Style Fish, 109
  Oyster Bacon Wrap, 15
  Seafood Bisque, 57
  Shoyu Poke, 3
  Shrimp Curry, 103
  Shrimp Lumpia, 16
  Shrimp with Black Bean Sauce, 107
  Taegu Ocean Salad Linguine, 29
Seafood Bisque, 57
Sesame Seed Chicken, 11
Shortbread Cookies, 132
Shoyu Chicken, 95
Shoyu Poke, 3
Shrimp Curry, 103
Shrimp Lumpia, 16
Shrimp with Black Bean Sauce, 107
Soba Salad, 26
Sour Cream Chocolate Cake, 122
Spanish Rice, 108
Spinach Dip, 8
Spinach Rolls, 13
Spinach Salad with Hot Dressing, 27
Sponge Drops, 139

Spring Rolls, 9
Strawberry Salad, 28
Stuffed Aburage with Somen, 18
Stuffed Cabbage Rolls, 67
Stuffed Tofu, 110
Sugar Cookies, 140
Sukiyaki, 66
Sweet-Sour Spareribs, 77

T

Taegu Ocean Salad Linguine, 29
Takuan, 42
Tofu,
  Ma Po Tofu, 82
  Pork-Tofu Casserole, 81
  Stuffed Tofu, 110
  Tofu Burgers, 109
  Tofu Pie, 133
  Tofu Salad, 30
Tofu Burgers, 109
Tofu Pie, 133
Tofu Salad, 30
Tonkatsu, 74
Tri-Colored Mochi, 150
Turkey Chowder, 58

W

Watercress,
  Tofu Salad, 30
  Watercress Egg-Drop Soup, 47
Watergate Cake, 113
Won Ton Soup, 60

Y

Yakitori, 91

Z

Zucchini,
  Butter Yaki, 98
  Zucchini Cake, 158

Cooking

WITH SWEETLEAF STEVIA®

119
RECIPES
INSIDE

SweetLeaf™
Natural Stevia Sweetener

PICTURED: MINI FLOURLESS
CHOCOLATE CAKES P.101

Cooking with SweetLeaf Stevia®

Copyright 2014, Wisdom Natural Brands®

Various recipe contributions from Maya E. Nahra, RD, LD; Sugar-Free Mom; Cakes by Contessa; Pastry Chef Romina Peixoto; Pastry Chef Matthew Lodes; and SweetLeaf fans and employees.

Editing, cover and interior design by McFadden/Gavender Advertising, Inc.

Food photography and styling by Heather Gill

Wisdom Natural Brands
1203 West San Pedro Street
Gilbert, AZ 85233
800-899-9908
www.wisdomnaturalbrands.com

Printed in the United States of America

First Printed Edition, 2014

ISBN: 978-0-692-22495-3